They Weathered the Storm

The Banks/Baldwin and Allied Families

By

Clara L. Chandler

ISBN: 1-4107-2230-9 (e-book)
ISBN: 1-4107-2231-7 (Paperback)
ISBN: 1-4107-2232-5 (Dust Jacket)

Library of Congress Control Number: 2003091076

This book is printed on acid free paper.

Printed in the United States of America
Bloomington, IN

1stBooks - rev. 03/28/03

Table of Contents

Dedication

This book is dedicated to the memory of my loving parents, Herry Banks and Cora Baldwin Banks; my beloved brothers, Willie Lee Delk, Joe Clarence Banks, and Harry Cook Banks; aunts Mary Lee Sims, Julia Baldwin, Mary Baldwin, Alberta Banks, and Sallie Net Jones; uncles Luther Baldwin Sr., Eugene Baldwin, Edgar Sims, and Charlie Banks; cousins Carrie Mae Willis, Nellie Jones (Shug); and my beloved Johnnie Mae Lamar.

Acknowledgments

I truly appreciate all who have assisted me along this very exciting and spiritually fulfilling journey. If I had begun documenting ten years earlier, I certainly believe volume two would be necessary. Since, sad to say, my family has lost many of its grandest elders, my research depended upon the accounts of those family members whom I could speak with (including some who now have passed on), the National Archives, recorded census, and courthouse records.

First, I want to thank God, who guided me through this journey and allowed me to remain focused on the original intent of this book. And then, I am grateful for the heart-filled "baskets" of love, devotion, and respect given to me during the countless interviews. I want to thank my daughter, Barbara Banks, and son, Samuel Banks, who encouraged me to go ahead and jump with both feet first into deep, unknown waters of our family history. Thank you and I love you. I must note a special thanks to my husband, Hugh Chandler, for his patience, understanding, and support. Nikia Chandler has been my special helper in this adventure—my recognition of her and appreciation for her writing skills, encouragement, and all those hugs and kisses she gave me when I would reach an impasse.

Thanks also to Wayne Rorie for setting up my computer and to Ms. Montgomery for teaching me how to use the computer and remain organized. My thankfulness goes also to Verniece Rorie, who kept me motivated and lifted up in prayer. My appreciation to my sisters, Mary Stenson and Cora Ammons, and my brother, Hubert Banks, for sharing family memories. I thank Mattie Felton for her love and support, and I extend gratitude to Janie Jolly for sharing information she had collected through her research in Houston County, Georgia, and also for a picture she gave me of my great-great-grandmother Nancy Ross. Also instrumental in helping to provide information and support were my beloved Aunt Mary Sims, Uncle Ed, and Eunice Simmons, for their well-kept, detailed, bible records and pictures; Luther and Alice Baldwin for providing dates, places, events, and photos; and Johnnie Mae Lamar for her unselfish love and stories about the family. Lillie Simmons, Eva Simmons, Gladys Simmons, and Felton Jones also contributed with valuable input.

Although many letters were written, and numerous telephone calls were made, some people will be unintentionally left out—to them I offer my apologies. I have not strived for literary grandeur, but rather accurate family records. If my family finds these records acceptable, I have achieved my purpose. Herein, with my love, and through my best effort and memory, I give you some of the pain, happiness, humor, and wisdom of the past.

Foreword

<u>We are who we were!</u> Every person in this story is one of the pieces that compose our family history puzzle, which in turn is one piece with many angles in the giant puzzle of life. We each add shape, color, and nuance to this design as we walk down our life path, developing our character and relationships. We each are accountable for adding to the picture our integrity; honesty; ability to be slow to anger, but quick to forgive; and our willingness to nourish our friendships.

Other than for the Banks and Baldwins, this book may not be a bestseller, but it has the stature of being the first book published as a history on the Banks, Baldwin, and allied families. No matter whether you identify as being African American, Black, Negro, or a person of color, you must continue to stand firm and be aware of the danger we face by hiding our past. We must never be ashamed of the color of our skin or the sad truths about our ancestors being imprisoned on slave ships, treated as non-human—bought and sold like traded animals, and then isolated from the most basic human needs, a family bond.

Recognize that through these travails our forebears remained a strong people—people each of us can be proud of. We have a duty to teach our children that in ignoring and hiding the past we lose a part of our heritage, and doing so would inhibit healthy growth for our future. God loves us all. Yes, we struggled through the fight of self-identity.

We continue to fight. We divided a culture based on our color heritage. Some of us wanted to remain "Negro," others defined our culture by claiming African America, and others stretched to the fundamental extent of being "Black." We have allowed our past tragedy to set the tone of our future. Now as we settle into a new millennium, we as a people, no matter the skin tone, no matter of our past battles, no matter the injustices served to our ancestors, must continue to press forward harder and more determined than ever. Nor should we be so angered by the past that we think that all white people are bad. Let us instill character in our children, who are our future. God guided Moses (book of Exodus) in leading his people to the Promised Land. So I ask you, have we taught our next generation of people about the Promised Land and how to develop the character needed to get there? That is where our hope lies. My goal, in addition to relating the facts, is to write about particular life experiences. I want to capture and convey both the details of the family history and the spirit of the family heritage—our accomplishments, disappointments, joys, pains, trials, and triumphs.*

From my research, I have learned that often African Americans, particularly the elderly, didn't feel their lives were of value or that they made any contributions worth discussing or documenting, and they surely couldn't imagine that their lives would have any historical significance. I am reluctant to let that concept stand.

Introduction

I became interested in genealogy quite by accident. My husband's relatives were talking about having a family reunion. They had a lot of questions about who their ancestors were. I volunteered to go to the National Archives to do some research. In addition, my mother had just moved to Maryland from Florida because she could no longer take care of herself and live alone.

She talked about three granddaughters who were estranged from the family because of the unpleasant separation of their parents, and she had a burning desire to find them. That brought to my mind the movie *Roots* by Alex Haley. I decided that if Alex could find his family, then surely I could, too.

The idea lay dormant for about a year. Then, lo and behold, one day when I was sick with the flu and turned on *The Oprah Winfrey Show*, the program was dedicated to the topic of finding your lost loved ones. My heart started pounding because I knew this show would give me the tools I needed to find my nieces. That show changed my life instantly—my determination to find them was set in motion, and continued nonstop. Thank you, Oprah, for that show, and thank you Mr. Culligan for a well-detailed book (Joseph J. Culligan, *You, Too, Can Find Anybody: A Reference Manual* [Miami: Hallmark Press, 1994]).

I will begin this book with our ancestors, and end it with the most-recent descendants of the Banks and Baldwin families. *Please note that, per family members' request, documentation of birth dates are omitted to protect privacy. Birth dates have been included, however, regarding those who are deceased.*

To give justice to the full life story of each person in this book would take volumes. My focus has been twofold: One purpose is to depict some of the characters and times I knew best, and in doing so, hand down some of the flavor and lessons I gleaned from those people and years. The other goal is to set out the family tree to edify the younger generation.

Chapter One: Grandma Lizzie's Plight

According to the grapevine, my mother's grandmother, Lizzie Baldwin Perryman Smith (born 1874), was in her early teens when her first child (who became my mother's father) was born. She was said to have been a strikingly beautiful woman with very long hair. Although I couldn't find a marriage record during my research, I heard that she married a James Perryman when she was about twenty-five years old, and they had a son named Major and later another, James junior. People say she spent a great deal of time sitting on the front porch of the home her husband bought (on Scofield Street, a section of Pleasant Hill in Macon, Georgia). She enjoyed talking to her neighbors, and some who knew her well said she was somewhat of a busybody.

When Mr. Perryman died, Grandma Lizzie married a man named John Smith. Family members claim that during her marriage to Mr. Smith she lost the house purchased by her first husband. I don't know details; but, allegedly, Mr. Smith brought a bag of financial problems to the marriage. Shortly after the loss of the house, Mr. Smith died.

Grandma Lizzie then moved in with my grandfather; and later, she lived briefly with my mother and father until she found another place to live.

She suffered a stroke that left her partially paralyzed and unable to do for herself. On January 4, 1948, she died of congestive heart failure.

Youther Baldwin and daughter Cora Mae at age 16

Chapter Two: Grandpa Provides for the Family in his Inimitable Way

My mother's father, Youther Baldwin, was a farmer, which helped him keep food on the table even though he was often away from home—looking for a wife or a crap game. He was a big handsome man, a womanizer, who also had a love for gambling. That was after his first wife, my grandmother Dora Swift Baldwin, died. He had five children with my grandmother.

My mother, Cora Mae Baldwin, was the middle child born to Dora and Youther. Mama came into this world on December 22, 1909, in Perry, in Houston County, Georgia. She had only one sister, Mary Lee, and three brothers, Luther, Walter, and Eugene.

But when my mother was merely thirteen, their mother passed away. I had the pleasure of strolling down memory lane with my mother as she remembered her childhood; her eyes betrayed no evidence of how hard it must have been to grow up without a mother with whom to share her special moments.

In Grandma Dora and Papa's house, Dora was the disciplinarian, and although she was taken from them early, she had instilled in her children the credo to be kind, love one another, have respect, and always be obedient. Aunt Mary Lee was the oldest (twenty or twenty-one when her mother died), so she basically had to take care of the little ones. I imagine Grandma Dora's sisters and brothers helped out when they could, but it must have been devastating for Mama and her siblings to face the death of their mother so early in their lives.

Many times Mama said that her sister Mary Lee and their older brother, Luther, were truly the ones who held the family together—they were always there to wipe away tears when one of their siblings was hurt or sad, to talk and listen, and to help with schoolwork.

The family kept the house running by carrying in water from the spring for cooking and bathing. For washing clothes, they mostly used rainwater; but when it hadn't rained, they brought water in from the spring for that, too. They also brought in chips for fire starters, and firewood for cooking on the wood stove and to heat the house during the winter months. Then, too, the two of them made sure the little ones played in safe areas and were lovingly put to bed at night. Mary Lee did most of the cooking and cleaning.

Clara L. Chandler

Cora, (standing) L-R Walter, Mary Lee, Florene And Eugene

Mary Lee Sims   **Luther Baldwin, Sr.**   **Cora Mae Baldwin**

Walter L. Baldwin   **Eugene Baldwin**

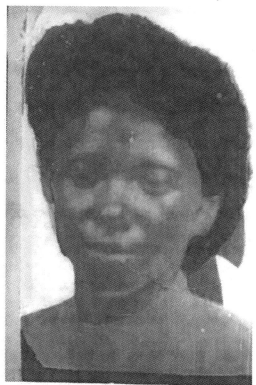

Dora Mae Ross Baldwin

Chapter Three: Daily Life in Cora Mae's Youth

Mama went to school in Houston County, and she was able to complete the seventh grade. She and her brothers—Luther, Walter, and Eugene—had to walk the five miles to school with books and lunch pail in hand. Most of the time they had holes in their shoes. Their father would cut pieces of cardboard to place inside the shoes, hoping to keep their feet warm and dry. During the winter months, the bitter winds would be so cold as to bring tears to her and her brothers' eyes, but they kept going, often crying all the way.

One day I asked Mama about the clothing people wore back in 1910 and 1920. With a faraway look in her eyes, she described dresses down to her ankles with long cotton slips, and said often a bonnet completed the ensemble. Mama and her friends didn't wear socks; instead they wore cotton stockings to school and church.

On weekdays when school was in session, the children had many, many chores to do before supper. When they had a chance to play— which was not very often—they mostly played with each other, because they were not allowed to play with or visit the children who lived nearby. families didn't let their children out of their sight for fear something would happen to them.

The reason was that in those days houses were built much farther apart than they are today, and the only times the children were allowed to play with each other was during recess at school or on Sundays in the churchyard—where the parents kept their eyes on them. Once in a while when adults visited each other, they would bring their children along and the parents would sit on the front porch catching up on community news and gossip while they watched the children play. When it was warm enough to play outside, Mama always played outside barefoot, and she was never allowed to go to bed without first washing her feet. Bathing her feet before bed became an obsession throughout her life.

During summer months, my mother and her brothers worked the fields, bringing in the crops, which were mostly collards, turnips, cabbages, pole beans, okra, corn, sweet potatoes, and peas. An advantage of growing up on a farm was that they didn't have to go to the store for vegetables; everything was grown right there.

Mama remembered her mother canning the vegetables in Mason jars and keeping them in the pantry, and also making jellies and jams from any available fruit. Times were hard, but Mother could not remember ever being hungry. Mama's sister Mary Lee, who was around fourteen or fifteen years old at the time, was always busy cooking, cleaning, or working. When she came in from the fields, she had to get supper on the table and tend to her baby brother, Eugene.

On Sundays, the children got to ride in the horse and buggy to church. Oftentimes the rain would come, but they didn't mind, as long as they were riding. The church services lasted all day with a break between Sunday school, morning, and afternoon services to allow them to partake of the food that parents would prepare on Saturday to be shared at church on Sunday: baskets of buttermilk biscuits, sweet rolls, sausages, fried fatback, and whatever fruit was in season. Everybody relished the meal between Sunday School and morning service.

Chapter Four: Youther's Transgressions

Every weekend Papa (the name we called our grandpa) and his friends would meet back in the woods to shoot dice (crap) and play a game called Skin. Most times Papa would come home with winnings between twenty-five to fifty dollars; Mama never heard of him losing much of his money. But then, one morning when Mother was around age ten, Papa returned after gambling all night, and he had literally lost his shirt off his back. He said it happened because he was trying to win back what he had lost, as he had nothing left to show for his week's work.

That did not stop him from going back a couple of weeks later, however. This time when he returned home, he came to the edge of the field and whistled for Grandma. When she came out, he was sticking his head out from behind a tree, and he asked her to bring him some clothing—he had gambled away everything on him, *including his clothes.* He had lost his pocket watch, hat, overalls, shirt, and even his shoes.

Grandma Dora fulfilled his request so that the children would not see his nakedness. Papa was mad at his friends and mad at himself for losing all his money, Much later, he was overheard telling Grandma that it was a fair game but he lost because he was down on his luck: Grandma told him he had lost because God did not approve of gambling.

Grandma often earned a few dollars sewing for different families in the area—she was good at it. I guess that helped put food on the table when Papa messed up. Also, they didn't spend a lot of money on things we do today, such as soap and toilet paper. Every outhouse had a Sears Roebuck catalog or some newspaper and you had a choice: Make use of it, or do what they did in biblical days—find a leaf. Sweet-smelling soap was unheard of back then; everybody used homemade soap (lye soap).

It was a severe episode of asthma that took Grandma Dora. A few years after Grandma's death, Aunt Mary married and moved to Macon, Georgia. By late 1930, the whole family had relocated to Macon, Georgia.

Grandpa (Papa as we called him) was always employed. During the summer months, he was the ice-man who delivered blocks of ice to people's homes to be used to keep their food from spoiling. Although the refrigerator was invented in 1803, times were hard and most families could not afford to buy one, so they used ice boxes.

When winter came, Grandpa was the coal man, delivering coal so

people could keep warm.

Nancy Swift

Chapter Five: The Baldwin's Native American Heritage and Pride, and Slave History of the Family

Mama's family (the Baldwins) was predominantly Cherokee, with a mixture of Blackfoot, Creek Indian, and African American blood. They were determined people—once they began something, they persevered until they finished what they had started, even though it might be difficult. They believed the family must stay together no matter what—that when someone is in trouble, you don't throw the person away; you stand by them. If they are family, they will always be family.

The Baldwins are assertive, spiritual, and compassionate. Their devotion shows in their attitude that the family praying together will enable it to stay together. The family members are very strong and high-spirited.

Another characteristic that seems rooted in the Native American heritage is their pride of hair—hair is *glory*. Mother was proud of her hair—all the Indians had that. The maternal side of Mama's family was all dark-complexioned, with thick hair, high cheekbones, and big noses. The (Swifts).

Only when I became an adult did I find out that Mama and Aunt Mary had different fathers. Grownups did not talk much about themselves, and we knew better than to ask. We were taught that children were to be seen and not heard. It was considered disrespectful to pry into adult affairs—of course, that never stopped us from discussing it with each other.

Mama was built solid and had shoulder-length hair and a medium-chestnut complexion, as did her brothers. But Auntie was petite and had a very fair complexion; her hair was black and silky, and it reached all the way to her waist.

I asked Mama who Auntie's father was, but she said she did not know. Auntie had the most beautiful pair of eyes—they seemed to sparkle when she laughed—and she had such a quiet spirit that it was very hard to anger her. In fact, I can't remember ever hearing her raise her voice.

Although the Baldwins lived in the era of slavery, they never mentioned anything about it. I learned more later while doing further research. I submitted this piece to *The Heritage of Houston County, Georgia 1821–2001* Publisher By,Walsworth Publishing Inc. *Exclusive Agent County Heritage Inc. Houston*

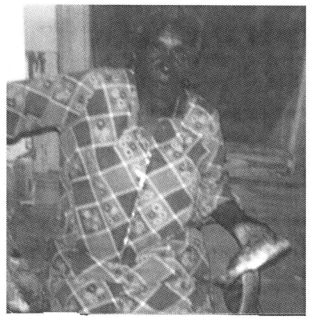

**Florene Henderson with
pride catch of the day**

Florene Ross was born in Perry Houston, Co. Georgia, She was 5'2"and 130 lb. A dark Chocolate skin woman with obvious Indian ancestry features. It is said that she had a mixture of Cherokee, Blackfoot and African American blood line. A kind gentle woman with a soft voice, she was a well-known and respected citizen and homemaker of Houston County, Georgia. Her parents Nancy Swift, born in 1863, and Enoch Ross, born in 1853 reared her. They lived, worked, and died in Houston County, Georgia. Her grandparents

17

Walton Swift and Harriet? Swift are buried in the Swift Cemetery in Houston, County. Her Great-grandparents were Wesley and Zenia? Swift. Wesley Swift and Zenia? were slaves. A slave owner named Harley/Hartly of Crawford County sold Zenia. She became the property of a Swift family in Houston County. No proof has been found on a marriage, but family information is documented that Zenia and Wesley had 4 boys and 3 girls, 2 girls died early, the 3rd was born with a cleft lip and was killed by the slave owner at birth. Two boys were sold to a slave trader from Dublin, Georgia. The last 2 boy's names were Walton and Alfred. Verbal Information states that Zenia lived past the age of 90, and Wesley died by drowning. Florene's aunts and uncles were Ford, Henry, Charles, Jane, Babe, J, and Edward Swift.

Florene Neal Henderson was a homemaker at the time of her death. She was 103 years old and lived at 702 Perimeter Road in Houston County Georgia.

Chapter Six: Papa Youther's Wife Hunting

Mother told me that a few years after Grandma Dora died, her father married a woman named Mabel, who was not much older than Mother. In fact, he got married about eight times after my grandmother Dora died.

I remember at least two of his wives. One was an older woman, named Mrs. Cora Searcy. I am sure that woman suffered from what we now call Alzheimer's disease. My grandfather would bring her to our house for Mother to take care of while he worked. This old lady would always seem to find a window or door to get out of and would wander away. My sister Cora and I would laugh—we were just children and had no idea of the serious problem this woman had.

If our mother had known we laughed at that old woman, we surely would have gotten the switch to our butts. Now that I look back, I think we actually were afraid of Mrs. Searcy. Our neighbor Mrs. Lillie Mae Howard or her mother-in-law, Mrs. Mahalia Howard, would go find her and bring her back to the house. Grandpa was married to Cora Searcy when she died.

The other one of Grandpa's wives whom I remember was named Pinkie. She could have earned a place in the *Guinness Book of World Records* for being the world's worst cook. If you cannot cook grits, that is a definite no-no to a Banks family member. Pinkie's grits were thick and lumpy; eating them was very hard because we were used to them cooked smooth—definitely without lumps. Grits was not the only thing Pinkie would make a mess of: She would burn the cornbread and scotch the beans. Once Papa told her to fix us a peach cobbler. Now, that crazy woman didn't even peel the peaches well, and she must have forgotten to put spice and butter in it, because it sure didn't taste like the ones my mother made. And, forget her biscuits—they were so hard that the chickens shook their heads at them.

Bless her heart, though, she did try. One thing she did well was to show Cora and me how to make strawberries and cream. Papa had strawberries growing on the fence in the backyard. They were big and juicy, and tasted really good with sugar and cream (pet milk in a can).

We knew better, however, than to complain because Pinkie would have told Papa that we were ungrateful, which would have made him very upset with us. She was much younger than Papa, and she had a serious drinking problem. In fact, she was caught climbing over a fence the day of Papa's funeral—trying to get to the bootleg house to buy liquor. She was indeed a piece of work.

We did not spend much time with Pinkie after Papa died. Mother and her siblings had a disagreement with her about a piece of furniture—a china cabinet—that they said belonged to their mother. Aunt Mary did end up with the cabinet; I believe my sister Mary has that cabinet today. After that big deal, they decided not to stay in touch with Pinkie.

Chapter Seven: Mary Lee's Two Husbands; Like Night and Day

As quiet and soft spoken as Auntie Mary was. I am sure there was a time when she must have raised her voice, because as Uncle Gene (Mother's brother Eugene) told me, her first marriage was to a beast of a man, Johnny Smith, who was as mean as a snake, very abusive, and a womanizer. Her second husband, Edgar Sims, was quite the opposite. He was a quiet man with a loving disposition. No matter what the situation was or how bad you were feeling, he could always make you laugh. Auntie Mary and Uncle Ed loved children, but they weren't able to conceive any.

When Uncle Ed was 18, he had joined the United States Army (on May 15, 1918). He did his basic training in Fort McPherson, Georgia, and then served at Fort Gordon in Georgia, with Company F, Provisions Battalion, for ten days and then as Chauffeur/Vehicle Operator with the 873rd Company Transport Corps from May 25, 1918, to July 26, 1919. He received an honorable discharge as a private first class.

After serving in the army, Ed met and married Aunt Mary Later, they relocated to Florida, and Ed found employment with Armour Meat Packing Company in the early 1940s and remained with that company until he retired:

He started out as a delivery-truck driver. Then he advanced to work as a packer of sausages, bacon, hot dogs, and a variety of other meats. Later, he became a date-code inspector. By the time he retired, he was working in account receivable.

Aunt Mary's first husband had left her. He had been gone for many years, and I suppose they thought he was dead or never coming back. Ed and Mary decided to wed on April 10, 1943, in Jacksonville, in Duval County, Florida.

Little did they know that the first husband would return and try to ruin their lives. I understand that when he showed up to claim his wife, he was told by Uncle Ed that Aunt Mary could have been dead damned and delivered for all Johnny Smith cared, and that she was Ed's wife now. Mr. Smith did not put up much of a fight, because he could see that Mary was no longer in love with him and had moved on with her life.

Due to his return, the divorce was voided because it had been obtained by claiming that Mr. Smith was dead, and divorce proceedings had to be restarted. (Auntie Mary had actually thought he was deceased, and Uncle Ed didn't care whether he really was or not.) So, the best man won out, and Aunt Mary and Uncle Ed were remarried on March 18, 1963, in Charlton County, Georgia.

After they moved to a few places around Jacksonville, Uncle Ed built his precious Mae her dream home at 1630 West 35th Street in Jacksonville, Florida, where they lived very happily. They were faithful and active members of the First Corinth Baptist Church in Jacksonville from 1944 until their deaths.

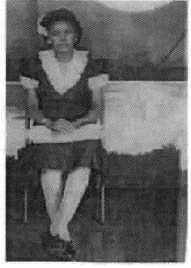

Edgar Sims   **Mary Lee Sims**

The home of Edgar And Mary Lee Baldwin Sims
1630 West 35th St Jacksonville, FL

Chapter Eight: Herry the Fix-It Man

My father, Herry Banks, was not well educated, but I do believe he was smarter than most people who only completed the third grade. Daddy was born September 22, 1907, in Knoxville, in Crawford County, Georgia, to Cook and Minnie Walker Banks. He was one of eight children—three girls and five boys: Charlie, Sallie Net, Joseph ("Joe"), Franklin, Homer, Ada, Minnie Lee, and my father (Herry). Daddy was a big, strong man with distinguished features attributable to his American Indian ancestry; like mother, he had some Cherokee forebears.

I can not picture him without seeing him in a hat—he never left home without one on—it was the first thing he put on in the morning and the last thing he took off at night. He loved his family. He also had a special love for food, alcohol, and working with his hands. Mama used to tell him "Herry if it is not broken, don't fix it," but he usually already had broken something so that he could put it back together. The neighborhood kids called him Mr. Fix-It.

He would often come home with something that someone had discarded, such as an old radio, electric fan, or broken chair. And when he finished with it, it was like new. He could actually look at something that needed repairs and not only tell you what was wrong with it, but also how much it would cost to fix it. He saved people a lot of trouble and money with what I consider a gift of self-taught knowledge and common sense.

Willie Lee Delk   **Harry Cook Banks, Sr.**

Joe Clarence Banks   **Mary Frances Banks**

Hubert M. Banks　　　**Clara Lucille & Cora Mae Banks**

The Home of Herry And Cora Mae Baldwin Banks

Cora Mae Banks Baldwin

Chapter Nine: Cora and Herry marry, Raise a Family, and Move around Macon, Georgia

My father didn't talk much about his childhood. I don't think he had that much of one. He mostly talked about work. Daddy was a very hardworking man. When he worked at Mckesson and Riley (in Bibb County), which was a drug-supply company, he was a stock clerk. At the time, Mama worked on an assembly line at nearby T & T Packing Company, a meatpacking company.

After a courtship of about eight months, Mom and Dad went to City Hall—and with each of their families' blessings, they were married in the town of Macon in Bibb County, Georgia, on February 22, 1928. Before my mother met Daddy, she already had a one-year-old baby boy named Willie Lee, who was fathered by someone she never talked about. Mama and Daddy named the first son they had together Harry (which is what everybody called my father, although my dad's name is Herry—not Harry. Many people misspelled it, and other people called him Henry, which Daddy hated).

There were nine members in my family: Mom, Dad, and the seven of us—Willie Lee, Harry, Mary, Joe, Hubert, Cora, and me. I didn't spend too much time with my two older brothers, Harry and Lee, when I was younger, but I have many memories I shared with Joe and Hubert.

Daddy's mother, Grandma Minnie Walker, moved in and was a big help to Mama while the babies were coming. In fact, she was the midwife who delivered five of Mama's babies; Cora and I were the only two born in the hospital.

Mom and Dad lived at various locations in Macon over the years: Harry was born when they lived on Tindall Avenue. They moved as the family grew, probably for more space. Joe Clarence was born on Pio Nona Avenue. Mary was probably born on Dempsey Avenue, as was Hubert. Cora and I were born on Straight Street; then the Board of Education bought that land, and the family moved to Poppy Avenue.

Chapter Ten: The Missing Moonshine

When my father was in a lighter mood, he would tell us funny stories and ghost stories. He recounted the story of one night (when he was somewhere between forty-five and fifty years old) when he took a shortcut through the graveyard while he was returning home from his friend's house:

He had bought a half pint of moonshine, and he stuffed the bottle into his back pocket for safekeeping. Out of nowhere, he heard footsteps, but he was afraid to look back, so instead he walked faster. The steps got louder and louder, so he took off running. Next thing, he heard a sucking noise. He ran as fast as he could, not stopping until he reached home. Once safe inside the house with the door locked, he reached for his bottle. To his dismay, it was broken to pieces in his back pocket.

He explained that a ghost had robbed him of his moonshine. Now, he reasoned that because he had not fallen and his pants weren't wet, the ghost must have hit his pocket, which broke the bottle, and then the ghost sucked up the moonshine that had leaked onto his clothing. Did we believe him? Yes, we sure did. But, of course Mama had a different opinion about what really had happened. She was very aware

of Daddy's immense enjoyment of drinking.

Chapter Eleven: The Routines

Mama worked as a domestic most of her childbearing years. She also took in washing and ironing for the rich white people around Macon to help her make ends meet. On washdays, a fire would be built under a big black kettle full of water. After the water was heated, it was poured as needed into the washtubs, where clothes would be scrubbed by hand or by using a washboard—the kind now seen mostly in museums. After the whites—sheets, pillowcases, all-white underwear, tablecloths, napkins, curtains, and the like—had been scrubbed with lye soap, they were placed in the big kettle to boil out the rest of the dirt.

Then Mama put the clothes and cold water into a No. 2 tub (a round, flat-bottomed tin vessel usually wider than tall but deep enough to hold twelve long-sleeved shirts or four bed sheets).

That same tub, by the way, was what I was bathed in. After the clothes were rinsed through this, they were put into a second tub of water for the final rinse. Then some were starched, while others were hung on clotheslines to dry.

They had better be clean, or the process would be restarted. A friend of mine remembered a time when she had hung clothes on the line, but they did not meet her mother's standard of cleanliness: "Blind" with rage, her mother pulled the clothes off the line, smashed them in the dirt, and yelled, "Don't put them back on that line until they are clean."

When Mama was growing up, her family neither had water in the house nor even a well nearby, so they had to haul water from a creek. Mostly they used it for cooking and sometimes for washing; generally, they depended on rainwater for washing and bathing. If you've ever heard of the old saying, "Don't throw the baby out with the wash water" that is exactly what this reminds me of. We literally bathed in the same No. 2 tin tub that was used for washing clothes.

I wondered where Mama learned her wonderful cooking skills. She said it was from her sister Mary, who learned from an old lady named Hattie Mae Phillips. Mama could bake buttermilk biscuits that would simply melt in your mouth. Her cakes were good, too. I won't take any credit away from my mother, but Aunt Sal Net baked the best cakes. People didn't use self-rising flour in those days (the early 1940s), and they didn't have electric mixers, but all the ingredients were fresh. One of our neighbors had a couple of cows, and we got fresh milk and butter.

Also, Mama raised chickens, so we had fresh eggs. I have met a lot of people who grew up in the south who say they don't eat grits, red-eyed gravy, or beans anymore, and don't own up to being from the South. Personally, I still enjoy a bowl of grits, and I love beans. One thing is for certain: My parents taught me that I could make a better life for myself, but I should never forget where I came from. My father was grateful for my Mama's cooking; his favorite foods were collards, turnips, kale, and mustard greens cooked with ham, with a bake sweet potato on the side.

Mind you, we were not dirt poor, but we were a far cry from having all we needed or desired. I recall times of having too little to eat and wearing hand-me-down clothing. Mama often made our dresses. The feed bought for the Banner chickens came in printed cloth bags, which she would turn into slips and pinafore dresses; sometimes she made curtains from the bags, too. I must admit the clothes were pretty, at least to my eyes as a child.

Winters were the worst times. Most people don't think of the south as a very cold place in comparison to Upstate New York,

Chicago, Colorado, or any of the colder states. I guess you can say

that's true, but you could have fooled me when I lived in Georgia.

Gas stoves, electric heaters—we had no earthly idea of their

existence. We had a wood stove in the kitchen that was used for

cooking.

My brother Hubert had the responsibility of keeping the fire

burning and replenishing the wood box for the next meal, which he

said was a very hard thing to do. We also had a fireplace in the living

room and potbelly stoves in the bedrooms. It amazes me to hear

people rave about the fact that they have fireplaces in their homes—

Well, whoopee! and to think they *choose* to have them today! In the

days of yesteryear, we had no other choice.

As I think about it, I don't believe we were any worse off than

anybody else in the neighborhood. Times were hard for everyone

back in those days. Slavery was supposed to be over, but it sure didn't

seem to me as though it was. Whites were still calling Daddy "boy"

and Mama "gal." I think Mama did the best she could with what she

had, and I assure you that what she had was not much.

Thank God she learned how to make quilts, because she certainly

didn't have extra money to buy those beautiful blankets she saw in the

Sears Roebuck catalog, and we definitely needed heavy covering to keep us warm during those cold winter nights when the fire went out. Mama loved three things—her children, her husband, and quilting. When she was not tending to her children or in the kitchen cooking, you could find her, next to a pile of material, finishing a quilt or starting a new one. She called this her time of relaxation.

People very seldom were sick back then; when they were, home remedies made them well in no time, and quilts kept them toasty. I've often wondered whether Mama sewed quilts for the love of creating quilts or rather from the need to keep the children warm. I think both reasons apply. Mama's eyes would light up when she would speak about the beautiful quilts her mother, Dora, made. I guess that is who gave Mama and her sister the quilting bug.

They continued my grandmother's tradition—transforming scraps from dresses, aprons, shirts, feed sacks, curtains, and tablecloths, or anything useful, into lovely quilts. I have one of the last ones Mama made before she passed. It is called "The Little Brown House." The background and border are white, with sixteen small brown houses as foreground, and the house in the middle of the quilt is slightly larger than the others, with a chimney. Each house has two windows and a

door. It's truly a work of art.

Joe C. Banks and his dog Tippy

Chapter Twelve: Hunting in the Backyard for Dinner

Joe was the oldest boy still at home for a short time while I was growing up, until he chose to join the Army shortly after high school. Mama raised and sold Banner chickens; and when we didn't have enough to eat, Joe would wait until our parents left the house, and then he would venture out in the yard to catch a chicken. Meanwhile, the rest of us would scramble about in the house: making a fire in the stove, heating water to clean the chicken, and getting the skillet ready. Someone would land the task of plucking the chicken, and Joe would cook it. By the time our folks returned, we had full bellies and the kitchen showed no evidence of the mischievous activity that had just taken place.

Not to say that Mama didn't find out about it later. This woman had eyes behind her head; I do believe she could even see through a few walls to another room. Of course I didn't understand until later when I became a parent why it is called a mother's instinct to know when a child is doing something wrong or is in trouble. As my sister Mary explained in a speech at Unionville Baptist Church one Mother's Day, mothers are equipped with the instinct to distinguish their own baby's cry in a room full of crying babies. Mothers can iron a load of clothes, cook a full-course meal, darn socks, keep a child from falling out of a tree, and see each of her other five children outside playing—all at the same time.

When I was a youngster, the war had just ended, and people were really struggling to survive. Winter was the time for hog killing. The hogs were kept on a floor bed, which was a platform of planks on top of the earth to keep the hogs out of the mud, and they were fed special grain to clean their systems for the slaughter. Family and friends arrived early in the morning to participate in this horrible event. They heated water in that big black kettle in the yard. One of the men would shoot the hog and someone else would stick a knife in its throat to make it bleed so it would not be so messy when it was dressed and sectioned. I don't know who did what—we were not allowed to see this part. What we did witness was the hog being dipped in hot water and then hung up and scraped until all its hair was removed. The poor thing was cut up into sections. Although I don't remember seeing a smokehouse, I do remember Aunt Sal Net and Mama cleaning chitlins, and Uncles Charlie, William, and Claude attended these events.

Sometimes when we had fire burning in the fireplace in wintertime, we would bake sweet potatoes in the ashes and fatback in the skillet, or Mama would cook neck bones and cabbage in a pot and cornbread in the skillet. A whole meal prepared in the fireplace felt fun to me.

Aunt Sal Net taught us that to keep their crop from going bad, they would more or less bury it, as far as I could understand: They dug a hole and put potatoes, corn, cabbage, onions, and some other veggies in it; then they protected them with a thick layer of straw, which was covered with a plank of wood and then with dirt above that. I believe they called this banking.

MR. & MRS. LUTHER BALDWIN SR.
@ 734 PEBBLE ST.

734 PEBBLE ST. — (1974)

Chapter Thirteen: Christmas time

We had two Aunt Mary's, Mama's sister (Aunt Mary Lee Sims, married to Edgar) and Mama's sister-in-law (Aunt Mary Baldwin, married to my mother's brother Luther). Uncle Luke's Mary used to bake fruitcakes. She would keep them in the attic, which we called the loft back then, and once a month she would bring them down to pour wine or fruit juice over them to keep them moist. At Christmas, she always served fruitcake. Being at that house was always pleasurable.

Christmas was a really big deal to me when I was a child. We would jump for joy seeing all the shiny new toys and clothes Santa had brought us. On Christmas morning, after we said our prayers, we would head for little shoe boxes that were set out—one for each of us. Every box would have a toy or two, hard candy, apples, oranges, raisins, varied nuts, and something to dress up in. We had so much pleasure from it.

Family and friends would stop by, and we had a lot of food to eat. In the evening, we would go to Aunt Sal Net's house. It would be so warm—filled with relatives. We had food at our house, but we always loved being at Aunt Sal Net's, where we reveled in eating all kinds of cakes and pies. She almost never said no to us. If we already had cake

and asked for more, we got it.

Sallie Net Banks Jones

Chapter Fourteen: Herry and the Company Strike

When Daddy worked at Mckesson and Riley, the pay was very low. The workers often talked about a strike. After much discussion, they agreed on the day to strike. That day came, and everybody had second thoughts. They all ended up reporting to work—that is everybody except Daddy. Indeed, he got fired for not showing up.

After he lost the job, Daddy picked up odd jobs around the neighborhood: He could do plumbing work, electrical work, and he also made good money putting in cesspools for people who were installing bathrooms in their homes. At that time, a lot of folks were getting rid of their outside toilets. They were also having running water and electricity brought into their homes.

It didn't take Daddy too long to find a steady-paying job. He began working at the Central Georgia Railroad in the late '40s, laying tracks up and down the southern states. Although he had begun to make better money, he was drinking it up. As far back as I can remember, Daddy never passed up a drink. Until much later in my life, I wasn't aware that Mama took a drink now and then. Daddy was a guzzler, but Mama was a nipper—no comparison between the two.

Daddy worked for the Central Georgia Railroad for many years. After he left the Railroad, Daddy was called an everything, anywhere, anytime fix-it man. I can't remember anything he could not do. If it broke, he could fix it, and he often made extra money by fixing things in the community.

Chapter Fifteen: Boogie-Woogie and Boozing

On the corner of Anthony Road and Key Street (away from private homes) in Macon, in a big brown building, was a juke joint called The Music in the Tree. (I think they had speakers lodged in the tree to attract the crowds.) Another joint closer to us was called Collier's Place. Whichever one it was that the music came from, that certain boogie-woogie blues music would always set Daddy to doing the Buck dance when he heard it.

He must have showed the Buck Dance to all the grandkids, because they can still do it today. Especially Roslin—she can imitate him to a tee. Daddy frequented these juke joints, as well as a few others around Unionville. I remember Mae Bessie's place on Dempsey Avenue, Strick's on Poppy Avenue, Nell Bailey's Place, and Booker's Place, and I know there were more.

People went every Friday and Saturday night to listen to local musical groups, drink booze, dance, eat and mingle. Sometimes they sold fish, BBQ pork, and chicken dinners. Daddy would go to one or another of these joints and hang out drinking until the wee hours of the morning.

49

As he neared the house again, he would be singing songs from Muddy Waters, Lighting Slim, and John Lee Hooker. One of his favorite songs started like this, "Oh, baby, why don't you keep your big legs off of mine, cause you know it's three o'clock in the morning, and I ain't even close my eyes." We always knew what was going to happen when he got home. We learned to brace ourselves, prepared to spend another sleepless night. Daddy would wake us to tell who he saw, what they did, what he did, who died, who got locked up, and what he ate.

We were kept awake, too, by his loud singing until dawn. Sometimes Mama's trying to get him to shut up and go to bed would lead to an argument. Mama never won any of these arguments, because he just kept on singing and ignoring her. The family would shout for joy when his mood and booze wore off and he finally fell asleep.

Now Daddy was more than a basic weekend drinker: It was bad, and I do mean Bad with a capital "B." He was a pain in the butt on most weekends. Sundays were the worst because he'd start coming off his binge. That's when he'd begin the "bring me" syndrome—"bring me some water," "bring me something to eat," "bring me my shoes," bring me this, bring me that. I used to say to myself, "Why the hell can't he get it himself?" Of course, we would have been crazy to act like we didn't want to cater to him.

Daddy wore Brogan shoes most of the time. They smelled something awful, mama would put them out on the back porch so we didn't have to smelled them.

Chapter Sixteen: Summertime Explorers

Still, the family really enjoyed the years Daddy worked for the railroad. We were allowed to travel by train at a discounted rate, and sometime we received free passes. Mama's sister Mary Sims lived in Jacksonville, Florida. My sister Cora, my brother Hubert, and I took turns spending the summers there. Mama used to put us on the train with our little shoebox lunches, filled with sandwich, fruits, and peanut butter crackers. We would be so excited that when the train began moving we thought we were on our way and started eating our lunches. Much to our surprise, the train would only be backing out of the station, and we could see our parents still waving. We would laugh so hard about not knowing we were still in Macon.

Auntie Mary and Uncle Ed would meet us at the station in Jacksonville in their big, shiny brown Hudson automobile. As we walked into their house, the smell of fresh fruit always welcomed us; there was plenty food to eat. Uncle Ed was a darling man; we always got what we wanted from him—within reason, of course. They did not tolerate disobedience or nonsense. He knew we loved bologna, and he would bring a whole roll of it from work just for us. I am sure we messed over a lot of food while we were there—playing with it, or not liking and refusing it—but they never scolded us. Those were wonderful times.

We always went to church on Sundays, and every week we would visit the beach or go to the zoo. Sometimes Aunt Mary and Uncle Ed would take us fishing, or wherever we wanted to go. When we fished, we would catch drums, brim, and many other kinds of fish. (I used to think that shrimp was only used for bait—not itself something to eat.)

We mostly caught fish from off the bridge over the Saint John River, but sometimes we fished at the end of the beach.

Fishing from the bridge was scary, because people traveled on that bridge.

We were able to do it because the cars and trucks moved very slowly across and we knew better than to play in the middle. Aunt Mary and Uncle Ed would often come home from fishing with a good catch. Other days they would complain that the fish were not biting.

All the children loved to comb and brush Aunt Mary's hair. Uncle Ed used to say "Mae" (which was his pet name for her) "them young-uhs are going to give you the worst headache of your life if you do not get them off your head." She would say, "Ed, leave them alone, they

53

are not bothering me." When she saw him getting upset, she would tell us to go play, but she seldom pushed us away.

When she fixed her hair, she would either braid it in two plaits and cross them on top of her head or make a bun at the nape of her neck. Mostly the bun was done on Sundays for church, so she could fit one of her many hats to match an outfit she had made.

Auntie Mary and Uncle Ed were so good to us. They showered us with all the nice things we couldn't get at home. Unfortunately, they were unable to conceive any children of their own, so they helped Mama with us and also helped my Mama's brother Uncle Luke and his wife (the other Aunt Mary) with their children.

Aunt Mary worked as a domestic. During her own time, she enjoyed cooking, sewing, quilting, knitting, and crocheting—to name a few of her hobbies. And she generously entertained her nieces and nephews.

Uncle Ed died in 1971 after a long struggle with diabetes. Auntie Mary suffered a heart attack in 1982, and after receiving a pacemaker, she made a remarkable recovery. She passed away in 1985 from another heart attack.

Cora Mae Banks resting after catching the biggest fish of the day.

Mary Lee Sims fishing on St. John's River in Jacksonville, Flordia.

Milton Owens

Chapter Seventeen: Florene Henderson, my Grandaunt

Grandma Dora had a sister, who I remember well. She lived in Perry, Georgia, and her name was Florene Henderson. I heard that she gave birth to about five children but they had all died at birth or soon after. Her one remaining son is named Milton. He lived in Miami, Florida, for many years, and Aunt Florene was either traveling to see him, taking trips with the church, visiting family in Macon, or visiting my Aunt Mary Lee Sims in Jacksonville, Florida. She was always on the go.

Aunt Mary, Uncle Edgar Sims, and Aunt Florene loved to go fishing—and they were good at it, too. They would get up around five o'clock in the morning on those occasions. Upon returning home, they would cook squash with onion, make some corn bread, and cook enough fish for supper. This meal would be the culmination of the day: They would joke about the fish that were too small to keep and the ones that got away. They usually gave the rest of their catch to the neighbors or put the fish in containers and froze them with the heads left on—that was said to keep them fresh.

Aunt Florene remained active and healthy until she was past the age of 100. Only then did she begin to slow down. She died in her home state of Perry, Georgia, at the age of 103 in October 1991.

Chapter Eighteen: Hiding from the Insurance Man

Oftentimes Daddy made the money and brought it home to Mama, but he always seemed to find a reason to beg her for some of it back. If she refused, all hell would break out. When I was growing up, some of those times were chaotic amongst us. On paydays, Mom would have to meet Daddy down on his job if she intended for us to eat the next week.

She had to get to him before his drinking buddies did, or it was beg and borrow until next payday. Sometimes she didn't find him in time, and he would get so drunk that he couldn't make it home; he would either get locked up in the stockade or get robbed of all the money he had left after buying booze or giving cash away to others.

I cry remembering how very generous and, to a point, naive Daddy was. He thought everybody was his friend, when actually they were using him. After he'd sober up and realize what he had done, he would be so angry at himself. The sad part is he never could say no to his friends, so he repeated the same mistakes over and over.

My parents paid their life insurance to an agent who came to the house to collect payment. Often when that time rolled around, there would be no funds available, and Mother would be so ashamed she would send one of the children to the door to tell the insurance man that she was not at home. In fact, she would be hiding behind the door. I could never understand why she did that because, if he had tried to hurt our mother, my sister Cora and I would have locked our teeth into that man so bad that he would have been glad to leave that house with or without payment.

I remember times when the electricity was cut off because the bill wasn't paid, and Daddy would go to the box and turn it back on. It was only by the grace of God that he never got caught. He did the same with the water and gas.

Thank God for my big sister Mary and all my relatives who helped us weather the family storms. These were the times when Mother would have to get some housecleaning or clothes-washing and ironing jobs or baby-sitting to make ends meet. My sister Mary would take care of Cora and me, because these jobs kept Mama away from home all day and sometimes late at night.

Chapter Nineteen: Siblings; Mary Shoulders the Burden

Our home had two bedrooms, a living room, and a kitchen. My brother Hubert had his own bed; my two sisters, Mary and Cora, shared a double bed. My other brothers were already on their own out of the home. Me being the baby, I usually slept with Mom and Pop. Sometimes they lay me in the bed with my sisters, but they complained because they would always wake up cold and wet.

The memories of childhood bring back both tears of sadness and tears of joy, and then other memories make me laugh. We were raised to love one another and to respect our elders.

I used to think that the whole community was connected to my parents at the hip, because somehow our parents knew about everything we did or didn't do, and everybody would yell at us. Daddy was strict about who used the switch or belt on his girls, so I am told, but it didn't seem to matter much about the boys. Daddy was old-fashioned—he felt that if you were grown, you had to get out of his house and get your own. In other words, he was the only boss he wanted in the house. I guess it was kind of like the birds: When their young became a certain age, the mother bird would push them out of the nest, so they could learn to fly and feed themselves. In fact, it has been said that Daddy ran all the boys away from home.

I believe my sister Mary had the hardest time of all of us. She was given the responsibilities of caring for the younger children. Because Mama worked for a white family who was always in need of her services—cooking, cleaning, washing, ironing, or caring for their children—my sister was left to do for us. She helped us with our homework, washed and combed our hair, and washed and ironed our clothes.

Basically we were good kids, but we could be a handful at times. It was a bit much for her, especially because I was a whiner and was always fighting with Cora, our middle sister. Once when Mary was ironing, she was sitting on a stool as she usually did while ironing; however, this night she was so tired after doing her chores and her own homework that she fell asleep at the ironing board. The iron fell, burning her leg. She still has that scar today.

Mama and Dad were never the "hugs and kisses" type. Mary was always the one giving out the affection to us and wiping away our tears. The only time she seem contented was when she was reading her favorite magazines, *Modern Romance, True Experiences,* and *True Story.*

Mary did most of the weekday cooking, because Mama went to work. I don't remember whether Cora or I had to help cook, but I certainly remember having to take out the pee pot. Doing the dishes, either Cora or I would wash and the other would be responsible for drying the dishes and sweeping the floor. Without fail, we would fight about whose turn it was to wash—neither of us wanted to do it. I was actually the lazy one who would cause the fighting.

Looking back, it all seems so silly now. I often find myself crying and wishing I had those days back: My sister Cora often disagreed with me as most sisters do. I liked to play house and make mud pies, she liked to run, jump, play ball and climb trees. I was timid while she had a fiery temper. She could get angry very quickly. Hubert told me he remembered one morning before school my mother was outside talking to a neighbor and had forgotten to kiss Cora goodbye. Cora became very upset, refusing to go to school until mama gave her a kiss. She has changed over the years, probably because she is now a mother. I would gladly wash *and* dry dishes just to be able to be near my sisters. I used to hear the older people say, "You don't miss your water until the well runs dry." That is an understatement. Now, we

have all grown up, married, and have separate lives, with some great

distance of miles between us; but I thank God for the telephone.

Rosalee Ross Lane

Willie Lee Delk

Cora & Herry Visiting Lee on a visit to see Willie Lee in Sing Sing Prison.

Chapter Twenty: Willie Lee Goes AWOL

My oldest brother, Willie Lee, was in the army, and when he came home on a pass, he decided that he did not want to go back. The military police began looking for him, and Mama sent him off to Uncle Luke on Pebble Street in Tindall Field (then a section of Macon, Georgia), where he hid from the police. I guess they thought the police would kill him. After the MP did not find him, late one night Uncle Luke sent him on a train to Mama's Uncle Frank, who lived in New York City. (Uncle Frank was the ex-husband of my mother's Aunt Rosa Lee.

Willie Lee remained in New York until he died. My brother Hubert, my sister Cora, and I never got to know him well because, unfortunately, he got into trouble in New York and was sent to Sing Sing prison for a very long time. I haven't been able to learn details about the charges against him.

He must have gotten out in the late 1950s, because that is the first time I saw him to remember him. I was pregnant at the time and Willie Lee (whom we called Lee) asked if he could name my son; we took the name he chose, Jerome, as my son Samuel's middle name.

Lee met and married a wonderful woman named Florence. They were happy until he met up with an old girlfriend from back home and began an adulterous life with her. He became an alcoholic who made drinking money by drawing portraits of people on the subway. The sad truth is he was so good at drawing that he could have become an artist had he applied himself. He remained with the old girlfriend until he died.

Robert Neal, Herry Banks and John Neal

Chapter Twenty-One: A Scary Night Moving from Here to There

We lived next door to Unionville Elementary School. As a child, I looked at this school as big. But apparently it was not big enough—because the board of education wanted to expand. And in 1948, when they made the decision to expand, the board offered Daddy a fair price for the land on which our house stood. (I think they paid between six to seven thousand dollars). Daddy purchased a lot on Poppy Avenue just around the corner.

He had a lot of friends with good home-remodeling skills. They all showed up to help Daddy move the house. It proved to be a good thing that he worked at the railroad, because he was able to get crossties, chains, cables, most everything he needed. The lot where they planned to put the house was on a hill.

The move took three days to complete, and the city blocked off our street during the process. The house actually was moved with all the furniture still in it, and as we could not afford to go sleep in a hotel, Mary, Hubert, Cora, Mama, Daddy, and I lived in the house during the move and slept there during the nights. When they started moving the house, Cora, Mary, and I were so afraid.

One night Cora and I woke up screaming because we heard a loud squeaking sound that seemed to be coming from under the house. We were told that one of the cables that was holding the house was slipping loose, and the house was moving with every squeak.

The next thing we knew, Mr. Bennie Howard—a neighbor across the street—came running, yelling for Daddy. I guess he had heard the squeaking noise, too. I imagine he was afraid for his family as well as ours, because we had a very long electric extension cord stretched from an outlet in their house to ours for light: otherwise, we would have been in the dark during the nights. That extension cord might very well have popped and started a fire. Lord knows I will never forget Mr. Bennie—this kind-hearted gentleman actually saved our lives.

During that three-day house-moving ordeal, plaster fell off the walls, furniture was damaged, and we had to eat a lot of cold food and the next while, but we also had some good, cooked meals. People came from everywhere to help us settle in. Of course Daddy could have done most of the work on the house himself, but it would have taken a long time. We had bricklayers, plasterers, electricians, and lots of bodies that could do anything that was required to make our house livable. Daddy's friend Robert Neal and his brother, John Neal, were his bricklayer buddies. Many others helped, but I've forgotten their names.

An outhouse served our purposes on Poppy Avenue, until a septic tank was installed. If my memory serves me correctly, Daddy put that in, too. We weren't afforded the luxury of an inside bathroom, equipped with tub and basin, until two or three years later. We would bathe in a No. 2 tub in the kitchen—yes that same No. 2 tub we used for washing clothes. Daddy had to do the kitchen over due to the damage during the move, and he also built an extra bedroom and dining room.

Chapter Twenty-Two: Industrious Hubert

My brother Hubert had his niche of jobs in the family. He always had to get up early and make a fire in the stove so Mama or Mary could cook. Hubert used to sell newspapers, first selling a paper called the *Pittsburgh Courier,* which carried mostly Black people news and sold for fifteen cents; later, he sold the *Grit News* for ten cents. During the summer when he was about fourteen or fifteen years old he awakened early—around 4:30 in the morning—to catch a truck to Unadila, Georgia, where he picked cotton. He was good at harvesting cotton. In fact, he could pick two rows at a time, and he always brought the money he made home to Mama to help out. Most of what he purchased for himself was a few comic books, which he enjoyed reading and swapping with his friends.

A quiet young man, Hubert never bothered anybody. Nevertheless, sometimes he would forget to do a chore, such as sweeping the yard or cutting the stove wood. At those times, Daddy would get the belt and threaten to whip him. Well, that was a hard job for our father, because as soon as he would mention whipping, Hubert would take off running, and Daddy could never catch him. Hubert

72

was the same way about taking medicine, such as the castor oil our parents would give us every winter to keep us from catching colds. No one could ever hold Hubert long enough to get a dose in him—luckily he very seldom got sick.

When he hit teenage years, during the school year he worked evenings at a drive-in restaurant with his best friend, Bobby Hunt. My sister Cora and I would wait up for him every night because he would bring us cheeseburgers and milkshakes. Hubert played football as a linebacker for his high school, Ballard Hudson—that is, until Mama saw a football game. She put a stop to that for fear he would get hurt.

Hubert recalled one time he and Mary had been given bikes for Christmas. On a day when Daddy had to go to town to pick up his pay check from the railroad, he rode Mary's bike and Hubert rode his bike. Well, my father met up with some friends downtown and got to drinking. He told Hubert to stand by the taxi stand until he would return. The sun lowered; it was after six o'clock in the evening, and Hubert was ready to go home.

When he went to look for Daddy, he found the police with him, jacked up and ready to go to jail for being drunk in public. Hubert did not know what to do, because he couldn't get both bikes back home.

73

A lady named Eleanor saw him standing there visibly upset. She knew him and also knew that our Uncle Walter worked at a furniture store nearby. Off she went to find Uncle Walter, who came and took Hubert and both bikes home.

I think Mama was so mad at Daddy that she let him stay in the stockade for two days. His fine was ten dollars or ten days. Of course, by this time he was broke and didn't have ten dollars, so off he went to jail.

Chapter Twenty-Three: A Teacher Who Changed My Life

Some time later, I came down with a bad case of whooping cough and later contracted rheumatic fever. The doctors advised my parents to put me in a school for the handicapped so that my activities would be monitored. I was sent to the new school, which neither allowed me to participate in any sports nor allowed me to play like the other children my age. And I lost contact with most of my friends. I was angry and devastated by the transfer. As a result, I became withdrawn at school and rebellious at home.

About nine of us in our class had this dreaded rheumatic fever. Today only two of us are still alive. It is only by the grace of God that I am here. The other survivor is a prominent minister, still living in our home state of Georgia.

I must interrupt my story about our family right here to mention a teacher I had at this new school: Her name was Mrs. Monica Sims; she had also been my third-grade teacher and transferred to the new school when it opened. She was a great inspiration to me, and she helped me adjust. One day she made it a point to tell me, "In order to go forward and not fail, you must first stop looking back and make the best of where you are today."

She said that nothing is ever so bad it couldn't be worse—the outcome all depends on how you choose to live your life, and she suggested that if I would play and laugh with the other children, my life would improve. I had been looking down on them because I saw them (all six other students in my class had rheumatic fever) as handicapped, but I didn't see myself that way. They cried and whined. My mother said, "You're better than them; make the best of the situation where you are." Now I see how sad it is that I looked down on them, and I'm sorry about it.

Some other sage words from Mrs. Sims were, "Trouble is always around the corner, and when it comes, it could very well be your own fault how you deal with it." For example, if I kept feeling that I was better than the other kids and kept playing with the healthy children, I might have fallen and hurt myself. She also explained that "if you have faith and determination to do good, most problems can be solved. Always remember that the difference between a good day and a bad day is your attitude."

Her words have influenced my life: If I try to do something knowing full well that I can't, I stop and meditate about it, and I have to come to grips with loving myself enough to admit I can't do something. If I feel that I can and it doesn't work, it's not that I failed—I gave it my best shot, and I move on. Working with developmentally disabled people, I know there are some things they can't do, but I don't shelter them as their parents do. Mrs. Sims's teaching reminds me to encourage them to do the best they can.

Mrs. Sims and my cousin Evelyn Walker went to college together, taught at the same school, and they still keep in touch. I got Mrs. Sims's address from Evelyn, and when I wrote her a letter, she responded with surprise that I would remember her after forty years. Now, she has reached the age of 84, which is a testimony to God's grace.

Chapter Twenty-Four: Can't Live With Him and Can't Live Without Him

On Poppy Avenue, Daddy had started selling moonshine out of our house. His drinking was a big problem for my mother in their marriage. Once my parents had a fight during which Daddy broke Mama's arm. I'm not sure what the fight was about, but I think it involved a man who frequently visited to buy moonshine. After that fight, my parents separated: My mother left my dad. This was not the only time she had left—there were many times before this, but Daddy always convinced her to come home by promising to never hurt her again.

My cousin Gladys tells me that I lived with her for one weekend when I was about four or five years old; I was 12 when Mary went away to school. More often than not when Mama left, Cora and I would be sent to live with a different relative. This time, Cora and I went together to Grandpa's house in the Pleasant Hill section of Macon. Grandpa was not a joy to be around—all he did when he was home was sleep.

I remember that his wife of the moment was Pinkie, who actually was the last of the seven wives he had since Grandma's death in 1922. We didn't stay with them that long, perhaps a couple of months.

Cora and I were very scared because our parents had come to the point of talking about a divorce, but meanwhile my father came to get us and took us to live with his sister Sal Net. She was kind and gentle. She had moved to Macon from Moran, Georgia, back in 1946, and lived with us until she took an apartment on Cedar Street. (Later, in December 1949, while she was living in the apartment, it burned to the ground. Luckily, she was unharmed.)

We loved the time staying at her apartment; for one thing, she could cook better than anybody else in the family. If you were in her neighborhood, you could always tell which house was hers by the smell of a good meal cooking. I loved suppertime: Aunt Sal Net always cooked greens and made corn pones. She was a pro with cooking greens, no matter what kind they were—collards, mustards, turnips, kale or watercress. Turnips were the best because she would make dumplings and cook them right on top of the greens in the same pot. One thing that sticks with me about her was that, unlike Mama, Aunt Sal Net was always home.

Shug (her daughter) was always there, too. Shug had a baby boy we called Bubba (his real name was Robert Hill Jr.). I had a hard time getting along with Shug because she was so bossy. I always wanted to play with Bubba, and she would scream at me to leave her baby alone. I used to dress him up at least three times a day, and tried to braid his hair, which he had very little of. Nonetheless, I would tape a ribbon on his head, and all hell would break out when Shug saw that. "I will be glad when Uncle Herry and Aunt Cora Mae come and get these younguns," she'd exclaim, and she'd yell, "My baby is a boy not a girl, get away from him before I hit you with my shoe. I am so sick of you trying to make him be a girl." Those were her favorite words.

During that time people used kerosene lanterns for light, and Shug would always blow out the lantern to keep me from finding the baby at night—I hated her for that. I protested to Mama that Shug was the meanest "old" woman in the whole wide world.

Gladys Jones   Simmons Nellie Mae   Jones Felton Jones

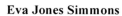

Robert Jones, Sr.   Eva Jones Simmons   Joseph Jones

Anne Moten & MaryM. Baldwin   **Ruth K. Mays**

Mathis Kleckley

John Mosley (Sonny)

Chapter Twenty-Five: Retreating at Luke and Aunt Mary's

I hated Daddy, too, because he was mad at Mama, and kept us from home. From Aunt Sal Net's we went to my mother's family. We stayed with her oldest brother, Uncle Luke (Luther), and his wife, Mary Mims Baldwin, at their home on Pebble Street. They were good people and good to us.

In our young minds, we thought they were rich, because their children always got what they wanted. They provided well for us, too, such as buying us new clothes for school and church. They didn't have much of a front yard, but in the little space Aunt Mary had, she grew beautiful flowers. If I remember correctly, their backyard was large, so that is where we played.

Uncle Luke was a man among men: He had a loving disposition, and his eyes were always open to the funny side of life. All my mothers siblings pretty much were, and Uncle Walter still is, very slow to anger, never raising their voices—actually, you could never tell when they were angry. Uncle Luke was a hardworking, quiet, gentle soul, and he was devoted to his family.

Annie told me that Uncle Luke used to have a club called The Moonglow and another store or club that I have forgotten the name of. Oftentimes he would come home from work and find a few extra little feet under his table—most times, those would be the feet of the Banks children. He never seemed to mind, and there was consistently plenty of food to go around. You could always find Uncle Luke when you needed him. Yet he was very active in his church and community.

Luke was a very kind person and treated all people with love. He never laid fault at my Dad, never said anything like "Why did you hit my sister?" His wife, Aunt Mary, would get angry at Daddy and say things, but Uncle Luke would say "You can't see what happened behind that bedroom door when he closed it." He was a sanctuary for all of us. So loving.

To be near their children during his retirement years, Uncle Luke and Aunt Mary later relocated to Philadelphia, Pennsylvania, where he also became very active with the church and neighborhood association.

Carron, & Carrie Willis and Luther Baldwin, Jr.

Johnnie Mae Lamar

Chapter Twenty-Six: Aunts, Uncles, and Cousins Come Through

The only siblings of my mother who had children were Uncle Luke and Uncle Walter. I recently heard that Walter has a son, Curtis Baldwin, who lives in Riverside, Ohio. Most of Uncle Luke and Mary's seven children were grown and out of the house by the time we stayed there. But one of the girls shared a lot with me, including some of the information in this book: Her name is Annie (everybody calls her Sweet). Uncle Luke and Aunt Mary also raised two grandsons, Mathis and John (who we called Sonny). Mama described the wedding of one of the girls—Lois, I think it was. The wedding was held at the house, and so many people attended that they feared the floor would cave in.

Then there was Uncle Luke and Aunt Mary's daughter Ruth, who was a nurse and a hairdresser: She always did our hair for special events, such as church programs and school plays. Those were horrible days for me. My sisters' hair would look good for days, but mine would be a total mess the same day it was set. My hair has a softer texture than Cora and Mary's hair; and it was (and still is) long and has a mind of its own. So many times it would drive me to tears. Another one of their daughters, Johnnie Mae, would try to reassure me with "Don't cry. One day you will have a hair style that everybody will be jealous of." Well, that day has not come yet, but I promised myself that when I would be grown up, I would cut it and do whatever I want with it. I am still trying different styles. I've cut it several times during my adult years; for now, I like it long again.

We never spent too much time with Uncle Gene and Aunt Julia. Since she was still fairly young and didn't have any children, she liked to party a lot. Yet, when we came to her house, she was always glad to have some children around and to play with us. She showered us with love and also bought us gifts. Gene was a tall, slim, handsome, and fun-loving guy, who never looked his age. I guess that was because he was born in a leap year, or maybe it was his genes. All the ladies fell head over heels when he entered a room.

We spent some time with Uncle Walter and Aunt Rebecca. Her mother, Mrs. Zollie Brantley, and Mrs. Brantley's adopted daughter, Maggie, lived with them. Once when I was playing baseball in their yard, I missed the ball and hit a beehive in the tree with the bat. Those yellow jackets swarmed all over me. Mrs. Brantley put some medicine on me, but I wanted to go home right then. I was a mess—they'd gotten my head, neck, and face. I healed quickly, though, without the trip to the doctor that most people would do nowadays.

The one person who always knew where Mama was, was her brother Walter. If any occasion arose that we needed her, all we had to do was call him and he knew where she was.

MEMORIAM
MRS. JULIA MAE BALDWIN
In loving memory of my dear wife who departed this life July 3, 1979. Sadly missed by husband, Mr. Eugene Baldwin and other loved ones.

Rebecca Brantley Baldwin

Chapter Twenty-Seven: Mary's First Date

My sister Cora and I still have laughs about Mary's first date. I think the whole neighborhood knew about that. She and her date were going to the movies. They had to ride the bus, which meant they had to walk from our house on Poppy Avenue, to Dempsey, and then up a long street called May Avenue to Columbus Road, which was the closest bus stop to get them to the Douglas or the Roxy Theaters. I don't know how all the people found out about it—but then, I guess I do, because everybody knew everybody else's business. Still, it was amazing to learn that the old folks were sitting on their front porches and the young ones were hanging out windows to get a look at the Banks girl on her first date. To this day, I can't imagine why she wanted to date this guy. I don't want to sound mean, but not only was he short and fat, but he was ugly, too. God forgive me for that.

Mary's best girl friend was Olivia McKay: That girl laughed all the time. They are still best friends—so is Lettie Marcus, and her two sisters, Johnnie Mae and Dorothy. I think Lettie was Mary's "big sister" when she was in nursing school.

Chapter Twenty-Eight: Entering Womanhood, Reluctantly

By the time the changes came for me—that transition from an innocent little girl to a know-all teenager—my sister Mary had gone away to college to study nursing. We really missed her, for she was the only one who kept us in line. I hit puberty very early. I was in Sunday school when that awful day arrived.

There I was, wearing my best baby-blue dress, and walking toward the line at the offering table, when a lady pulled me out from the line and asked me if my mother was home.

I said, "No my mother is at work."

"Do you know what to do?" she asked.

I lied saying "Yes," so she sent me home. I don't remember many details of that day, but I do remember crying for my mother and trying to wash the blood away.

Finally later that evening, Mama came home and told me as little as possible about what was happening to my body—just enough to assure me that I was not dying and that this happens to all girls. It didn't take me long to get all the details after I told a few girls at school. Of course most of the information I received had nothing to do with the truth of the matter. These were the times I missed my big sister; I am sure she would have set me straight.

Mary Frances Banks

Chapter Twenty-Nine: Mary Pursues Her Dreams

Although she never said so, I bet Mary was glad to go away to school (in 1953). She desired to become a nurse. After having to take care of us, I could not imagine why she *chose* to go into the medical field. With the help of Harry, one of the older boys who had moved away, she attended nursing school, and she continued to go to college after college after that, earning degree after degree—even after she married and began her own family.

One of the saddest times of my life was when I couldn't attend her graduation from nursing school. The graduation ceremony was held ninety miles away in Atlanta, Georgia, and I was under my doctor's advice not to travel because I was in my sixth month of a very difficult pregnancy.

She came home from nursing school and was married on our front porch, with Cora standing next to her and Marshell Stenson Jr. (the groom) next to his brother Nathan. Today Mary is a very happy wife and mother with a successful career. She has a wonderful family, and a marriage that I am sure God created before she was even born. I am so proud of her.

The only difference with Mary today is that she has so many pairs of shoes she has a hard time deciding which ones to wear. When she was growing up, she didn't have that choice, because she only had one pair. In fact, I think she shared that pair with my brother Hubert. For that and many others things, I say *"Thank you, Jesus."*

Willie Mae Harge   **Joe Clarence Banks**

Chapter Thirty: Joe Clarence Banks, the Lover of All Time

Joe was the lover of all times, at least he thought he was. He dated a girl named Gloria, who lived in Florida, and she had a daughter with him, born September 22, 1953, and given the name Katherine.

Two years later, I remember he had two girlfriends at the same time, Pearl Jones and Willie Mae Jones (not related), and I truly believe he loved them both. At any rate, they both had a child for him. Pearl gave birth to a son born September 8,1955, whom she named Clarence. Willie Mae gave birth to a daughter born September 24, 1955, whom she named Diane. The family knew about the two in Macon—Diane, and Clarence—but didn't learn about Katherine in Florida until some years later. Of course Mama and Auntie Mary did know and, for some god forsaken reason, kept it to themselves.

When Joe moved to Brooklyn, New York, in late 1955, he met Dorothy Williams. They fell in love and were married in 1956. Three daughters blessed their marriage: Rebecca Gayle, Dorothy Jean, and Vivien Denise.

For reasons unknown to me, Joe and Dorothy's marriage went sour around 1963 and Joe moved to Atlanta. They parted on unfriendly terms, and, although the couple never legally divorced, the family was denied the privilege of seeing the girls.

Mama never gave up hope. A few years later, Joe passed away, and my mother was determined to find these children and to help their mother Dorothy get Joe's social security benefits. Mama accomplished that goal, but although the break up had nothing to do with my mother, Dorothy still held on to the bad feelings. We lost contact with the girls.

Herry And Cora Mae Baldwin Banks

Chapter Thirty-One: Herry and Cora Mae Get It Back Together

Mama's and Daddy's families both gave Daddy such a hard time about his drinking that he started to straighten up because nobody wanted to be bothered with him, plus he missed his family. We all begged Mama to take him back. Finally, he convinced Mama that he was going to do better by her and us kids. And he did—for a long time. I don't remember when he began acting up again; but, by this time Mama had decided to make a go of their marriage and raise her children as best she could, taking the good with the bad. Their marriage improved as they aged. They even took a trip to England together for their forty-fourth wedding anniversary.

On weekends, Daddy and Mama mostly went their separate ways. Mama was in a circle of people who played bid-whiz at a different house every week. Bid-whiz is a card game that people play with partners. You bid on a hand you think is a winner. A deuce of spade is a wild card, and one person begins a suit with the others playing a higher card of the same suit to win. Your partner is supposed to watch you and play according to your hand.

The game was played in a circle; that is, Mama would host the game one Saturday and someone else would host the next Saturday. The game would go around to each member's house until it was again the turn for the first person. The host would cook food and have music, just among themselves. If you weren't in the circle, you were not allowed to participate, because each member in the circle paid dues and that money was used to purchase the food. It was considered bad manners to invite an outsider.

Mother knew a lot of people—both men and women—but mostly men. I hated all of them, because in my young mind I felt that they were taking her away from home. Only when I grew up did I realize that she went to get away from us and it was her time to be with her friends.

Herry Banks

Chapter Thirty-Two: Herry and Cora Move to the Big Apple

There was a big change in Macon during the civil rights movement: People stopped riding the buses, and the younger groups began sitting at the food counters at the "five and dimes" stores as well as using bathrooms marked for whites. Boycotting and sit-ins occurred all over the South.

Harry had moved to New York some years earlier, and I think he feared that something would happen to Mom and Pop during those unsettled times. He talked them into visiting him in Brooklyn in the hope they would move there; they liked New York and decided to sell the house in Macon. That was in 1963—a sad year for the United States—the year our beloved President John F. Kennedy was slain.

Daddy was happy to be reunited with his sons Harry, Hubert, and Lee, and also those old friends from home, John and Robert Neal. Hubert and his family had moved to New York a few years earlier for him to find better employment.

After some adjustments, Dad seemed glad to be there: He was able to obtain employment as a superintendent for two 20-family buildings. And, he was offered an apartment in one of the buildings.

Making a lot of new friends came easily to him—in fact, I don't think he ever met a stranger; he seemed to feel as though he knew everyone he met. Very friendly and kindhearted, he always seemed to me a bit too trusting. He often loaned people his tools—hammer, pliers, saw, screwdrivers, and the like—which they never returned. To make matters worse, he always provided the drink with people who never shared with him or offered to buy him a drink, and he loaned money to people who never repaid him.

Usually, he purchased his liquor from a particular store, and was well known there, to the point where he could purchase a bottle on credit. If he didn't feel like making the trip to the liquor store, he could send anybody with his hat: The store owner recognized it and would send him a bottle.

Knowing this, his friends often took advantage of this protocol, and sneaked his hat out with them when they wanted a drink, leaving Daddy with a big bill to pay. Most of the time he was content, doing the things he liked doing—that is, fixing things. But he was also sad

at times, because he missed his family and friends back in Macon.

Chapter Thirty-Three: Events of December 1974

Some years later, since Daddy was basically in good health most of his life, it was a big surprise when he became ill. He never complained, but people that knew him knew something was wrong. He just wasn't his usual jolly self. The family passed it off as his being lonely and missing Mama (because she had gone to Florida to see Auntie Mary). But, one Friday in early December 1974, when I was thirty-four, around noon a neighbor who lived on the first floor and had just come home from shopping saw Daddy just sitting at the bottom of the steps

When she approached him, he did not respond to her, which was very unusual. She came running upstairs screaming that something was wrong with Pop (which was the name all the neighbors used for my dad). She ran in with tears in her eyes to tell me that Daddy was downstairs sitting on the steps and she could not get him up. I went downstairs to see what his problem was. With one look into his eyes, I knew he was not drunk, so I asked him if he was sick.

He said "No baby, I am just too tired to make it upstairs. I just need to rest here for a minute or so." I asked the neighbor, Mrs. Betty, to keep an eye on him while I went to call my brother Harry. After I explained the situation to him, Harry said not to try to move Dad or make him get up, and Harry said he would send one of his employees, Joe Worrell, to take Daddy to the doctor. We took him to the doctor, who sent him to the hospital right away.

There he was hospitalized for abdominal discomfort. Mama came home from Florida and learned that Daddy had been hospitalized at Kings County Hospital in Brooklyn, New York. She spoke with his primary doctor who informed her that, after many tests and X rays, he was diagnosed with pancreatic cancer.

Surgery was unsuccessful. my father was discharged to come home, because a team of doctors stated that there was nothing else they could do for him. Mama and I did the best we could to make him comfortable, but the pain was too much for him to bear; shortly after Christmas we had to admit him into Wyckoff Hospital. He stayed with us a few months after surgery. Then, in Wyckoff Hospital at 3:10 a.m., on April 22, 1975… without saying goodbye… he slept his way into his eternal home.

Rebecca Gail Banks, Clarence Jones Banks, Dorothy Jean Banks

Diane & Dana Harge

Vivan Denise & Bill Marbury Jr.

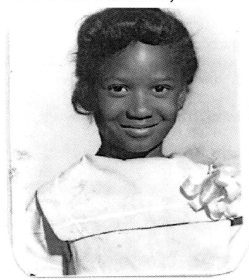

Katherine Banks

Chapter Thirty-Four: The Search for the Three Missing Granddaughters

When I began doing my research, I wrote letters in search of Joe's children, who we had lost touch with for thirty years. I contacted all the places that give public information: The Department of Motor Vehicles in Raleigh; North Carolina; the Brooklyn, New York, Board of Elections, the Department of Vital Statistics of Atlanta, Georgia; and the probate court of Jacksonville, Florida.

I tried everything suggested in Joseph Culligan's book, *You, Too, Can Find Anybody.* Finally, I hit pay dirt when I received a reply letter from North Carolina, where one of the girls had moved. I knew it was about Gail, but I felt frustrated and uncertain because the birth date on the copy of the driver record was incorrect and I was afraid I had the wrong person. It showed the same city and state as the one where her mother was born; and, with the exception of the year, it had Gail's correct date of birth. Little did I know she had changed the year to get her driver's license early. My gut feeling told me that this was one and the same person. When I sent for her to come to Maryland

and meet Mama, she admitted to having changed the year of her birth to obtain her driver license early.

One day when I was upset about not finding Joe's daughters, my nephew Harry junior called (he called me often since Mama had moved in with me in 1991). Because his mother and Dorothy were friends when he was growing up, I asked him when he had last heard from them. He didn't remember because they had moved and gotten married. He said his mother's telephone book was burned up in a fire, but he had stayed in touch with an older stepbrother of theirs, and he offered to try to locate a number for me.

About a week later, he called with three numbers. By this time, I had found more leads on Rebecca Gayle, the oldest girl. I called the numbers, and one was the number for Dorothy, their mother. She told me where the other two girls were: Dottie Jean was in Hagerstown, Maryland, less than a two-hour drive away; Gayle was in Chapel Hill, North Carolina, less than five hours away; and Denise was in Germany (where her husband was stationed in the U.S. Army.

Right away I left for Hagerstown. Since Dottie Jean was at work, I went to her job, where I recognized her instantly. We spent the rest of the day hugging and crying. When I returned home, I made arrangements to get Gayle and Jean to my house to meet their grandmother.

Denise was contacted in Germany, and we got to talk with her. About a year later, her husband, who was in the Army, passed away from a heart attack, and she brought him home for burial. She has since moved back to the States.

The child who was born in Florida was still missing, so by now I was going full speed ahead to find her, which was becoming harder each passing day, because research is not an inexpensive undertaking and my finances were limited. Joe has one son, named Clarence, and he was just as determined as I to find his sisters. I solicited his and his wife's financial help to find Katherine. He purchased a book called *The Locator: The Complete Guide to Finding Family, Friends and Loved Ones,* by Virgil L. Klunder and Troy W. Dunn. (Cape Coral, FL: Caradium Publishing, 1992). Many letters were written, and finally we had proof of where she was living. Her driver record led me to her in California, but that state has a privacy act that does not allow you to receive any information without the consent of the party in question, so I had to write her a letter addressed to Department of Motor Vehicles, which they forwarded to her. Fortunately, she called.

Unfortunately, the day in April 1997 that she called is the day I had returned home from Mama's funeral.

My husband noticed that the caller ID was full and the answering machine was full. And just as he finished saying that someone was really trying to get in touch with us, the telephone rang. Yes, indeed, it was Katherine. We both screamed with excitement. The next few moments were very painful for Katherine and me— it was very hard to tell her that she would never get the chance to see her grandmother, and I could hear the sadness in Katherine's voice. I desperately wanted to be near her, to hold and comfort her.

I told her that mother had memories of seeing her when she was a baby, and that her father had a picture of her in his wallet when he died. Katherine wanted to know about her family, and I wanted to hear more about her and her family, but the conversation was too emotional at that time, with both of us crying tears of elation; so after about half an hour of this, we agreed to talk more the next day. The timing was unfortunate, yet joyful. I called my sisters Mary and Cora, my children Barbara and Jerome, and my brother Hubert. I also called Katherine's sisters Diane, Gail, Dottie Jean, her brother Clarence, her cousins, my friends, and other relatives to tell them the good news, and to share telephone numbers and addresses. It was blessing and a dream come true to have finally made contact with each other. We have spoken often and have shared letters and family photos since that day, but as of this writing, time and money have not allowed us to meet face to face.

I hope that by the time this book is finished the Banks and Baldwin families will have a long-overdue family reunion date in place, and our ancestors can look down from the heavens and smile, knowing that the storms they weathered were not in vain. The elders are all gone now except Uncle Walter. And we thank God for him. He is still wrapped in the warmth of his faith. As we go forth with our lives, we must always remember that God is ever present and he can do anything but fail. To the younger generation I say, Not all is written in this book. Many more chapters exist. Talk to your parents, ask questions, document and document, and keep the Banks and Baldwin lineage intact.

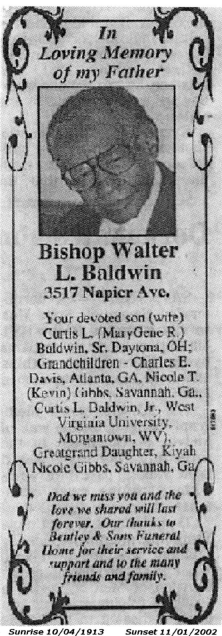

In
Loving Memory
of my Father

Bishop Walter L. Baldwin
3517 Napier Ave.

Your devoted son (wife) Curtis L. (MaryGene R.) Baldwin, Sr. Daytona, OH; Grandchildren - Charles E. Davis, Atlanta, GA, Nicole T. (Kevin) Gibbs, Savannah, Ga., Curtis L. Baldwin, Jr., West Virginia University, Morgantown, WV), Greatgrand Daughter, Kiyah Nicole Gibbs, Savannah, Ga.

Dad we miss you and the love we shared will last forever. Our thanks to Bentley & Sons Funeral Home for their service and support and to the many friends and family.

Sunrise 10/04/1913   Sunset 11/01/2002

Thank you Dr. Mary B. Stenson & Mrs. Marygene Baldwin for remembering the love.

LIST OF DESCENDANTS

Note: Each person is listed with the first name of the men who were their direct forbearers in parentheses, in sequence of the earliest generation to the most recent.

DESCENDANTS OF NEWTON BANKS

Generation No. 1

Newton Banks. He married **Sarah "Sallie" Jones.**

Children of Newton Banks and Sarah Jones are:

Cook Banks, born September 1865, in Knoxville, Georgia; died in Monroe County, in Georgia.

Benjamin Banks.

Generation No. 2

Cook Banks (Newton) was born September 1865, in Knoxville, Georgia, and died in

Monroe County, Georgia. He married **Minnie Walker** February 8, 1889, in Knoxville,

Georgia, daughter of **Frank Walker** and **Henrietta Lockett**.

Notes for Cook Banks:

Cook Banks was united in holy matrimony with Anna Jones in Crawford County, Georgia, on January 4, 1883. I found no information indicating how his first marriage ended. His second marriage—to Minnie Walker—took place in the same county. The 1920 census documents him, his wife, and children living in Knoxville, in Crawford County, Georgia. Relatives state that he is buried in an unmarked grave in the Smith Cemetery, which also is in Crawford.

Vital records of Atlanta, Georgia, and the probate court of Crawford County documented his death as February 22, 1922. The information on his death certificate is limited to name, date, time, and place—no cause of death is indicated. In all probability, he died before completed documentation of Blacks was required; of all the information researched about him, no records indicated slavery, and according to the birth date listed in the census of 1865, more than likely he was born a free man.

Notes for Minnie Walker:

Minnie was known to be a midwife. She moved to Macon, in Bibb County, Georgia, to live with her son Herry and his wife, Cora Mae Banks, in the late 1920s. She is buried in the Unionville Cemetery, which is located next to the Old Unionville Baptist Church on Pio Nona Avenue, in Macon. Her gravesite is easily found: It is approximately twenty steps to the left from the entrance and is a flat granite slab bearing this inscription:

Minnie Banks died Jan. 17, 1940

Henrietta Walker

Winston Walker, Jr. May 17, 1922–July 15, 1965

Avery Walker died Mar. 22, 1950

Winston Walker, Sr. died Dec. 5, 1939

Fannie Bryant Mar. 11, 1925–Aug. 9, 1994

A memorial stone marked *Evelyn Walker* is an open grave as of the date of this research (December 27, 1998)

Children of Cook Banks and Minnie Walker are:

Charlie Banks, born October 18, 1889; died October 20, 1953, in Knoxville, Georgia.

Joseph Banks, born October 1890; died 1930.

Homer Banks, born August 1893; died 1957

Franklin Banks, born November 1896; died 1929

Sallie Net Banks, born December 26, 1898, in Knoxville, Georgia; died December 29, 1989, in Macon, Georgia

Ada Banks, born 1903; died from a sleep disorder between 1930 and 1938, in Bibb County, Georgia. No information known of a spouse or children. Date of death and place of burial are unknown.

Minnie Lee Banks, born 1906; died 1946.

Herry Banks, born September 22, 1907, in Knoxville, Georgia; died April 22, 1975, in Brooklyn, New York.

Generation No. 3

Charlie Banks was born October 18, 1889, and died October 20, 1953, in Knoxville, Georgia. He married **Alberta Parker** on October 20, 1912, in Knoxville.

Notes for Alberta Parker:

Children of Charlie Banks and Alberta Parker are:

xx Banks, twin boys born June 19, 1913, in Crawford County, Georgia; died June 19, 1913. The boys were stillborn or died within minutes after birth.

Velma Banks, born February 19, 1914, in Knoxville, Georgia; died February 23, 1985, in Knoxville, Georgia.

Josie Bell Banks, born December 13, 1915, in Knoxville, Georgia; died January 11, 1967, in Knoxville, Georgia.

Charlie Banks Jr., born in Knoxville, Georgia.

xx Banks, born May 1, 1919; died May 1, 1919 (stillborn).

William Thomas Banks, born March 6, 1921, in Knoxville, Georgia; died May 4, 1973.

Eunice Lee Banks, born Knoxville, Georgia.

Lillie Mae Banks, born in Crawford County,

Georgia.

Claude Banks, born November 11, 1928; died May

22, 1967.

Homer Banks (Cook, Newton) was born August 1893; died 1957.

He married **Savannah Smith Gray**, daughter of Tom and Elisa

Gray. <u>Notes for Savannah Smith Gray:</u>

Savannah Gray had five children. Her first two daughters were

fathered by Homer Banks. The names of the other three were:

Elisa Gray

Tom Gray

Sarah Smith

Children of Homer Banks and Savannah Gray are:

Louise Banks

Bertha Banks.

Sallie Net Banks was born December 26, 1898, in Knoxville, Georgia, and died December 29, 1989, in Macon, Georgia. She married **Leslie Jones**, son of Mark Jones and Hettie Hart. He died September 9, 1944.

Notes for Sallie Net Banks:

She was a loving mother of six, and a good friend and neighbor to her community. She was devoted to her Smith Chapel Baptist Church family, which she joined in her youth. In 1928 she united with White Springs Baptist Church, where she served faithfully until her health failed.

On Friday morning, December 29, 1989, at 7:30 a.m., just two days after her 91st birthday, without saying goodbye, she placed herself up for offering and was gone. We knew in our hearts that her job here on earth was over, and her journey to her heavenly home was now at hand.

The epitaph was given that begins with, "A precious one has gone …"

Farewell services were held Tuesday, January 2, 1990, at White Springs Baptist Church, in Lizella, Georgia. Burial site is in the church cemetery.

Children of Sallie Banks and Leslie Jones are:

Robert Jones, born April 29, 1921, in Crawford County, Georgia; died April 21, 1993, in Macon, Georgia.

Nellie Mae Jones, born April 2, 1923; died May 18, 1992, in Bibb County, Georgia.

Gladys Jones

Eva Jones

Felton Jones

Joseph Jones, born November 26, 1934; died January 1996 in Cleveland, Ohio.

Minnie Lee Banks was born 1906 and died in 1946.

Notes for Minnie Lee Banks:

Minnie married a **Mr. Clark** (first name is unknown). She was killed in a northern state by a jealous lover (not Mr. Clark), whose name is unknown. She had a son called Short Man, whose real name was **Ernest Evans;** his father was **J. D. Evans**. No date of death or place of burial is known.

Child of Minnie Lee Banks and J. D. Evans is:

Ernest Evans

Herry Banks was born September 22, 1907, in Knoxville, Georgia, and died April 22, 1975, in Brooklyn, New York. He married **Cora Mae Baldwin** (daughter of **Youther Baldwin** and **Dora Ross**) on February 28, 1928, in Macon, Georgia.

Notes for Herry Banks:

Herry was educated in the Crawford County school system. He joined the Ebenezer Baptist Church in Macon under the leadership of Reverend E. Riley.

Employed at Mckesson and Riley for sixteen years, he met his bride-to-be there, Cora. Later, he worked for the Central Georgia Railroad a number of years. After moving to Brooklyn in the early '60s, he joined Bethel Baptist Church under watch care.

The epitaph given is the one that begins with "I expect to pass through this world but once …," by Stephan G. Rellet

A funeral service sacred to the memory of Herry Banks was held on April 25, 1975, at Bethel Baptist Church in Brooklyn, New York. His burial site is located in the Evergreen Cemetery, Redemption

Section, grave No. 13056. An upright gray granite tombstone with a

cross reads:

1927 Lee Delk 1968

1907 Herry Banks 1975

1928 Harry Cook Banks 1990

As noted above, a stepson preceded him in 1968, and my father's

firstborn went after him in 1990.

Children of Herry Banks and Cora Baldwin are:

Willie Lee Delk, born March 31, 1927, in Bibb County, Georgia;

died December 3, 1968, in Brooklyn, New York. He married Florence

Jackson in Brooklyn.

Notes for Willie Lee Delk:

He was stepson of Herry Banks. His biological father is Willie

Alfonzo Lee Delk.

Notes for Florence Jackson:

Her children from a previous marriage are Donna and Jason.

Harry Cook Banks, born April 18, 1929, in Bibb County, Georgia;

died June 26, 1990, in Brooklyn, New York.

Joe Clarence Banks, born December 9, 1932, in Bibb County,

Georgia; died December 3, 1969, in Futon County, Georgia.

Mary Frances Banks, born in Bibb County, Georgia.

Hubert Manuel Banks, born in Bibb County, Georgia.

Cora Mae Banks, born in Bibb County, Georgia.

Clara Lucille Banks, born in Bibb County, Georgia.

Generation No. 4

Velma Banks (Charlie, Cook, Newton) was born February 19, 1914, in Knoxville, Georgia, and died February 23, 1985, in Knoxville. She married **Willie B. Moran** on August 26, 1940.

Children of Velma Banks and Willie Moran are:

Fred Moran.

Ruby Moran.

Willie Benjamin Moran.

William Thomas Moran.

Ossie Mae Moran.

Obie Moran.

Olivia Moran.

Clara Moran.

Clara L. Chandler

Josie Bell Banks (Charlie, Cook, Newton) was born December 13, 1915, in Knoxville, Georgia, and died January 11, 1967, in Knoxville. She married **Robert Henry Moran** on October 26, 1940.

Children of Josie Banks and Robert Moran are:

Mary F. Moran.

Frances Moran.

George Leon Moran.

Harry James Moran.

Jimmy Lee Moran.

Karren Moran.

Willie Gene Moran.

Robert Moran.

Charlie Banks Jr. (Charlie, Cook, Newton) was born in Knoxville, Georgia. He married **Estella Davis** on May 9, 1942.

Children of Charlie Banks and Estella Davis are:

Charles Thomas Banks.

Leroy Banks.

Annie F. Banks Johnson.

Dolly Banks Lawson.

Jessie Clyde Jones Banks.

Lillie Mae Banks Mays.

William Thomas Banks (Charlie, Cook, Newton) was born March 6, 1921, in Knoxville, Georgia, and died May 4, 1973. He married **McKine Evelyn** in June 1952.

Children of William Banks and McKine Evelyn are:

Lois Banks Allen.

William Banks Jr.

Charlie Leon Banks.

Curtis Banks.

James Banks.

Emma Banks.

Eunice Lee Banks (Charlie, Cook, Newton) was born in Knoxville, Georgia. She married Larkin James Simmons on October 24, 1946.

Notes for Eunice Lee Banks:

No children were born to this union.

Lillie Mae Banks (Charlie, Cook, Newton) was born in Crawford County, Georgia. She married **John Henry Simmons** on October 6, 1945.

Children of Lillie Banks and John Simmons are:

Diane Simmons.

Ralph Simmons.

Robert Simmons.

Patricia Simmons.

Deborah Simmons.

Claude Banks (Charlie, Cook, Newton) was born November 11, 1928, and died May 22, 1967. He married **Betty Evans**.

Children of Claude Banks and Betty Evans are:

Gloria Banks, born July 11, 1957; died April 20, 1996.

Claude Banks Jr.

Larry Banks

Etta Banks

Claudette Banks

Allen Banks

Arsonjia Foster,

Bertha Banks (Homer, Cook, Newton).

Children of Bertha Banks are:

Mary Lee Reid.

Delores Williams.

Leon Jones.

Norris Jones.

Richard Jones.

Robert Jones (Sallie Net Banks, Cook, Newton) was born April 29, 1921, in Crawford County, Georgia, and died April 21, 1993, in Macon, Georgia. He married **Mattie Reid**.

Notes for Robert Jones:

Robert was united in holy matrimony with **Carrie Jackson** until she passed away. Six children were born to this union. Realizing the need for a personal Savior and an eternal home, Robert joined the Smith Chapel Missionary Baptist Church in Musella, Georgia. From his loyal dedication and fervent service, he became a member of the Deacon Board and a Wardman. He also was a member of the Seven Wonders Society.

At the onset of World War II, he was drafted into the United States Army, and after serving his country diligently for four years, he was honorably discharged. Upon his return to civilian life, he found Civil Service employment at Robins Air Force Base, where he worked until he retired. At the time of his death, he was married to **Mattie Pearl Reid**.

Robert's homegoing celebration was held April 25, 1993, at the Smith Chapel Baptist Church, Route 1, Hopewell Road, in Musella, Georgia.

His burial site is located in the Springhill Baptist Church Cemetery.

No children were born to the union with Mattie Reid (second wife)

Children of Robert Jones and Carrie Jackson are:

Mary Jones, born December 31, 1942; died 1997.

J.C. Jones

Willie J. Jones

Robert Jones Jr.

Ceonia Jones

Lillie Jones

Nellie Mae Jones (Sallie Net Banks, Cook, Newton) was born April 2, 1923, in Crawford County, Georgia, and died May 18, 1992, in Bibb County, Georgia. She met and had a child with **Robert Hill Sr.**

Notes for Nellie Mae Jones:

I presented her son with a plaque, bearing these words from me—

<<<<<<<<<<<<<< GONE TOO SOON>>>>>>>>>>>>>>>>>>

Springtime April 2, 1923, marked the beginning of the life for Nellie Mae Jones.

Springtime May 18, 1992, God reclaimed this flower for his own garden.

<<<<<<<<<<<<<<<<<<<<<<<SHUG>>>>>>>>>>>>>>>>>>>

<<<<<<<<GONE TOO SOON< WAY TOO SOON>>>>>>>>>

<<<<<<<<<<<<<<<<<<<<<I'M FREE>>>>>>>>>>>>>>>>>>

In the service only. "I'm Free," by Linda Jo Jackson

Nellie's devoted son, Robert "Bubba" Hill Jr., and his loving wife, family, and friends bid their farewell at high noon, on May 23, 1992, at the Smith Chapel Baptist Church in Musella, Georgia. Her burial site is located in the White Spring Baptist Church in Lizella, Georgia.

Child of Nellie Jones and Robert Sr. is:

Robert Hill Jr., born in Macon, Georgia.

Gladys Jones (Sallie Net Banks, Cook, Newton) was born in Crawford County, Georgia. She married **Charlie Simmons**.

Child of Gladys Jones and Charlie Simmons is:

Mark Simmons. (Adopted)

Eva Jones (Sallie Net Banks, Cook, Newton) was born in Crawford County, Georgia. She married **James Simmons** on August 5, 1945.

Children of Eva Jones and James Simmons are:

Geneva Simmons, born in Musella, Georgia

Shirley Simmons, born in Knoxville, Georgia

Lois Simmons, born in Musella, Georgia

Johnnie Simmons, born in Musella, Georgia

Margaret Simmons, born in Musella, Georgia

Harold Simmons, born in Musella, Georgia

Charlie Simmons, born in Musella, Georgia

Larry Simmons, born in Musella, Georgia

James Simmons Jr., born in Musella, Georgia

Anthony Simmons, born in Musella, Georgia

Maxie Simmons, born in Musella, Georgia

Elnora Simmons, born in Musella, Georgia

Felton Jones (Sallie Net Banks, Cook, Newton) was born in Crawford County, Georgia He married **Ollie Jones**.

Children of Felton Jones and Ollie Jones are:

Gwendolyn Jones, born in Macon, Georgia

Felton Bernard Jones, born in Macon, Georgia

Renée Jones, born in Macon, Georgia

Joseph Jones (Sallie Net Banks, Cook, Newton) was born November 26, 1934, and died January 1996, in Cleveland, Ohio. He married **Josephine.**

Children of Joseph Jones and Josephine are:

Jackie Jones.

Teresea Jones.

Kacey Jones.

Tracey Jones.

131

Vickie Jones.

Harry Cook Banks (Herry, Cook, Newton) was born April 18, 1929, in Bibb County, Georgia, and died June 26, 1990, in Brooklyn, New York. He married **Emma Highsmith** in Brooklyn, New York, in 1969.

Notes for Harry Cook Banks:

His first marriage was in March 1956 to Alberta Jackson (born July 30, 1929; died 1991). Their marriage ended in divorce.

Two sons were born to this union:

Harry Cook Banks Jr., born in Brooklyn, New York

Curtis Alan Banks, born in Brooklyn, New York

Children of Harry Banks and Emma Highsmith are:

Christopher Darian Banks, born in Brooklyn, New York.

Natasha Decole Banks, born in Brooklyn, New York

Joe Clarence Banks (Herry, Cook, Newton) was born December 9, 1932, in Bibb County, Georgia, and died December 3, 1969, in

Fulton County, Georgia. He married **Dorothy Williams** in Brooklyn, New York in 1956.

Notes for Joe Clarence Banks:

Military—United States Army Reserve

ID/Rank—Private First Class, 1951; he served in the Korean War

Honorable discharge date—April 4, 1961

Purple Heart Medal (valor)

Medal of Honor (praise)

Joe fathered three children before his marriage to Dorothy Williams; they are listed below with their mothers:

Daughters	**Mothers**
Katherine Jordan born in Ferndenia Beach, Florida	Gloria Jordan
Clarence Jones Banks in Macon, Georgia	Pearl Jones
Diane Jones Harge in Macon, Georgia	Willie Mae Jones

Children of Joe Banks and Dorothy Williams are:

Rebecca Gayle Banks, born in Brooklyn, New York.

Dorothy Jean Banks, born in Brooklyn, New York.

Vivien Denise Banks, born in Brooklyn, New York.

Mary Frances Banks (Herry, Cook, Newton) was born in Bibb County, Georgia. She married **Marshell Stenson Jr.** in Bibb County, Georgia, on August 8, 1959.

Notes for Mary Frances Banks:

She earned degrees as a Registered Nurse and a Doctor of Education.

Notes for Marshell Stenson Jr.:

He became an ordained Baptist minister.

Children of Mary Banks and Marshell Stenson are:

Marshell Stenson III, born in Fulton County, Georgia.

Mary Adrienne Stenson, born in Fulton County, Georgia.

Timothy Emanuel Stenson, born July 5, 1966; in Macon GA died March 2, 1984.

Notes for Timothy Emanuel Stenson:

In his senior year of high school, Timothy—whose brief life was already full of success and promise—was killed in an auto accident while enroute to his home.

Joel Clarence Stenson, born in Macon, Georgia. He married Kartika Yvette Gray on March 14,1998, in Macon, Georgia.

Notes for Joel Clarence Stenson:

Joel and Kartika were united in the Lord Jesus Christ on March 14, 1998, in the presence of their parents, Mr. & Mrs. Leonard Gray and Reverend & Mrs. Marshell Stenson, in Macon, Georgia.

Hubert Manuel Banks (Herry, Cook, Newton) was born in Bibb County, Georgia. He married **Evelyn McMullin** in 1957, in Bibb County.

Children of Hubert Banks and Evelyn McMullin are:

Roslin Banks, born in Bibb County, Georgia.

Hubert Manuel Banks Jr., born in Macon, Georgia.

Ken Banks, born in Brooklyn, New York.

Cora Mae Banks (Herry, Cook, Newton) was born in Bibb County, Georgia. She married

Lamar Ammons, in Bibb County, Georgia, on January 27, 1968.

Children of Cora Banks and Lamar Ammons are:

Sharon Bonita Banks, born in Macon, Georgia.

Turonald Banks, born in Macon, Georgia.

LaWanda Ammons, born in Macon, Georgia.

MarVetta Ammons, born in Macon, Georgia.

Notes for Sharon Bonita Banks:

She married Jimmy Lee King; they have one daughter,

Kisa LeAnn King born in Columbus, Georgia.

Notes for LaWanda Ammons:

She married Willie Thomas on August 3, 1988, in Macon, Georgia.

Clara Lucille Banks (Herry, Cook, Newton) was born in Bibb County, Georgia. She married **Hugh D. Chandler** in Washington, D.C. on August 25, 1984.

Notes for Clara Lucille Banks:

Her first marriage was to Albert Burton Brown in Providence, Rhode Island Their marriage ended in divorce.

Children of Clara Banks are:

Barbara Denise Banks, born in Macon, Georgia.

Samuel Jerome Banks, born in Brooklyn, New York.

Generation No. 5

Robert Hill Jr. (Nellie Mae Jones, Sallie Net Banks, Cook, Newton) was born in Macon, Georgia. He married **Louise Smith** on January 23, 1971, in Macon, Georgia.

Children of Robert Hill and Louise Smith are:

Chevene Hill, born in Macon, Georgia.

Regenia Hill, born in Macon, Georgia.

Geneva Simmons (Eva Jones, Sallie Net Banks, Cook, Newton) was born in Musella, Georgia.

Children of Geneva Simmons are:

Jennifer Simmons.

Jermaine Simmons.

Shirley Simmons (Eva Jones, Sallie Net Banks, Cook, Newton) was born in Knoxville, Georgia.

Children of Shirley Simmons are:

Michael Simmons.

Tonya Simmons.

Janet Simmons.

Christie Simmons.

Willie Bernard Simmons.

Lois Simmons (Eva Jones, Sallie Net Banks, Cook, Newton) was born in Crawford County, Georgia. She married **Andrew Carter**.

Children of Lois Simmons and Andrew Carter are:

Angela Carter.

Andrea Carter.

Andre Carter.

Johnnie Simmons (Eva Jones, Sallie Net Banks, Cook, Newton) was born in Crawford County, Georgia. He married **Shelly Franklin**.

Child of Johnnie Simmons and Shelly Franklin is:

Kelisha Simmons.

Margaret Simmons (Eva Jones, Sallie Net Banks, Cook, Newton). She married **Elijah Askbrook**.

Children of Margaret Simmons and Elijah Askbrook are:

Demetria Askbrook.

Denise Michelle Askbrook.

Elijah Askbrook Jr.

Harold Simmons (Eva Jones, Sallie Net Banks, Cook, Newton)

Children of Harold Simmons are:

Nicole Simmons.

Stephanie Simmons.

Larry Simmons (Eva Jones, Sallie Net Banks, Cook˙ Newton).

Children of Larry Simmons are:

Larry Simmons Jr.

Brantley Simmons.

Cheryl Lynn Simmons.

Cierra Simmons.

James Simmons Jr. (Eva Jones, Sallie Net Banks, Cook Newton).

Children of James Simmons Jr. are:

Quantrell Simmons.

Grace Madelyn Simmons.

Evelyn Simmons.

Anthony Simmons (Eva Jones, Sallie Net Banks, Cook, Newton).

Children of Anthony Simmons are:

Antonia Simmons.

Antwan Simmons.

Antionelle Simmons.

Maxie Simmons (Eva Jones, Sallie Net Banks, Cook Newton).

Child of Maxie Simmons is:

Moniqua Eva Simmons.

Elnora Simmons (Eva Jones, Sallie Net Banks, Cook, Newton).

Child of Elnora Simmons is:

Nyundra Simmons.

Tonya Simmons (Eva Jones, Sallie Net Banks, Cook, Newton).

Children of Tonya Simmons are.

Joshua Daniely

Dionta Baker

Harry Cook Banks Jr. (Harry Cook, Herry, Cook, Newton) was born in Brooklyn, New York. He married **Lorraine Graham** in 1989.

Children of Harry Banks are:

Harry Cook Banks III

Ceasar Lemell Banks

Children of Harry Banks and Lorraine Graham are:

Brandon Tyler Banks

Sean Michael Banks

Curtis Alan Banks was born in Brooklyn, New York. He married Stacy Carter on October 8, 2000, in Brooklyn, New York.

Child of Curtis Alan Banks and Stacy Carter is:

Liza Marie Alberta Banks

Christopher Darian Banks (Harry Cook, Herry, Cook, Newton) was born in Brooklyn, New York.

Child of Christopher Darian Banks is:

Christopher Banks

Natasha Decole Banks (Harry Cook, Herry, Cook, Newton) was born in Brooklyn, New York. She married Wallace Junious

Katherine Banks (Joe Clarence, Herry, Cook, Newton)

Children of Katherine Banks are:

Claudia Banks Jeter

Clarence G. Banks

Jeffery Banks

Clarence J. Banks (Joe Clarence, Herry, Cook, Newton) was born in Macon, Georgia. He married **Althea Tillman** in 1980, in Warner Robin, Georgia.

Child of Clarence Banks and Althea Tillman is:

Charrod Javon Banks, born in Macon, Georgia.

Diane Harge (Joe Clarence Banks, Herry, Cook, Newton) was born in Macon, Georgia.

Children of Diane Harge are:

Dana Rashun Harge

Danielle Harge

Notes for Danielle Harge:

Adopted daughter of Diane Harge

Rebecca Gayle Banks (Joe Clarence, Herry, Cook, Newton) was born in Brooklyn, in in New York. She married **Jesse Alston**, in South Carolina.

Child of Rebecca Banks and Jesse Alston is:

Demeterius Rashon Alston.

Dorothy Jean Banks (Joe Clarence, Herry, Cook, Newton) was born in Brooklyn, New York. She married **Aaron Alston** on January 9, 1978, in Chapel Hill, North Carolina.

Children of Dorothy Banks and Aaron Alston are:

Nikki TeCora Banks

Antegia Sierra Alston

Shawn Christine Rice

James DaVale Banks

Vivien Denise Banks (Joe Clarence, Herry, Cook, Newton) was born in Brooklyn, New York. She married **Bill Marbury** in Germany.

Child of Vivien Banks and Bill Marbury is:

Bill Marbury Jr.

Marshell Stenson III (Mary Frances Banks, Herry, Cook, Newton) was born in Fulton County, Georgia. He married **Linda Dials**.

Notes for Marshell Stenson III:

He has a stepson, Christopher Dials.

Children of Marshell Stenson and Linda Dials are:

Marshell Stenson V.

Terrance Stenson.

Mary Adrienne Stenson (Mary Frances Banks, Herry, Cook, Newton) was born in Fulton County, Georgia. She married **Lansing Scriven Jr.** on July 2, 1988, in Bibb County, Georgia.

Children of Mary Stenson and Lansing Scriven are:

Jessica Frances Scriven.

Sara Jordan Scriven.

Charles Timothy Scriven.

Mary has one Step-son Tyler Scriven

Joel Stenson [Mary Frances Banks, Herry, Cook, Newton] He married Kartika Y. Gray on March 14, 1998.

Child of Joel Stenson and Kartika Gray is

Lauren Stenson.

Roslin Banks (Hubert Manuel· Herry, Cook, Newton) was born in Bibb County, Georgia.

Child of Roslin Banks is:

Ron Banks.

Hubert Manuel Banks Jr. (Hubert Manuel, Herry, Cook, Newton) was born in Macon, Georgia. He married **Leslie Anne Kelly** on February 15, 1997, in Salinas, California.

Child of Hubert Manuel Banks Jr. is:

Trevor Banks, born in California

Ken Banks (Hubert Manuel, Herry, Cook, Newton) was born in Brooklyn, New York.

Children of Ken Banks are:

Kenise Victoria Banks, born in Brooklyn, New York.

Krystyna Danielle Banks, born in Brooklyn, New York.

Sharon Bonita Banks (Cora Mae, Herry, Cook, Newton) was born in Macon, Georgia. She married **Jimmy Lee King** on September 10, 1982, in Russell County, Alabama.

Child of Sharon Banks and Jimmy King is:

Kisa LeAnn King, born in Columbus, Georgia.

Turonald Banks [Cora Mae, Herry, Cook, Newton]

Was born in Macon, Georgia. He married Elda Maria Martinez on Dec 15, 2001.

Child Of Turonald Banks and Elda Maria Martinez is: Jocellyn Rochelle Banks born in Fairfax, Virginia.

Barbara Denise Banks (Clara Lucille, Herry, Cook' Newton) was born in Macon, Georgia.

Children of Barbara Denise Banks are:

Sarrina Raysha Banks, born in Brooklyn, New York.

Louis Renda Banks Sr., was born in Brooklyn, New York.

Elijah Fard Washington, born in Brooklyn, New York.

Samuel Jerome Banks (Clara Lucille, Herry, Cook, Newton) was born in Brooklyn, New York. He married **Claudette E. Wilson**, May 25, 1985 in Brooklyn, New York.

Child of Samuel Banks and Claudette Wilson is:

William Marcus Banks, born in Hamilton,Ohio.

Clara L. Chandler

Generation No. 6

Harry Cook Banks lll (Harry Jr., Harry Sr., Herry, Cook, Newton) was born in Brooklyn, New York.

Children of Harry Cook Banks III

Rishona Aliyah Banks was born in Brooklyn, New York.

Malachi Aaron Banks was born in Brooklyn, New York.

Charrod Javon Banks (Clarence J., Joe Clarence, Herry, Cook, Newton) was born in Macon, Georgia.

Notes for Charrod Javon Banks:

Charrod met and had a son with Robin Warner.

Child of Charrod Javon Banks and Robin Warner is:

J'Von Marquis Banks, born in Atlanta, Georgia.

Charrod met and had a daughter with Janie Wooten.

Child of Charrod Javon Banks and Janie Wooten is:

Chaunie Janise Banks, born in Atlanta, Georgia.]

Demeterius Rashon Alston (Rebecca Gayle Banks, Joe Clarence, Herry, Cook, Newton) was born in North Carolina.

Child of Demeterius Rashon Alston is:

148

KeAngelo Alston, born in Washington, D.C.

Nikki TeCora Banks (Dorothy Jean, Joe Clarence, Herry, Cook, Newton) was born in Brooklyn, New York.

Child of Nikki TeCora Banks is:

Malik RaShande Jones, born in Hagerstown, Maryland.

Sarrina Raysha Banks (Barbara Denise, Clara Lucille, Herry, Cook, Newton) was born in Brooklyn. New York.

Child of Sarrina Raysha Banks and Guye Saunders is:

Omarri Khalil Saunders, born in Brooklyn, New York.

Louis Renda Banks Sr. (Barbara Denise, Clara Lucille, Herry, Cook, Newton) was born in Brooklyn, New York.

Children of Louis Renda Banks Sr. are:

Louis Renda Banks Jr., born in Jacksonville, Florida.

Isaiah Banks, born in Jacksonville, Florida.

Jasmine Denise Banks, born in Decatur, Texas.

Ron Banks (Roslin, Hubert, Herry, cook, Newton) was born in Brooklyn, New York.

Child of Ron Banks is Deron Ajalon Banks Dawkins, born in Richmond, Virginia.

DESCENDANTS OF LIZZIE BALDWIN PERRYMAN SMITH

Generation No. 1

Lizzie Baldwin Perryman[1] **Smith** was born February 1, 1874, in Madison, Georgia, and died January 4, 1948, in Macon, Georgia. She married **James Perryman**.

<u>Notes for Lizzie Baldwin Perryman Smith:</u>

The names of Lizzie's parents are unknown. The biological father of her first son, Youther Baldwin, is also unknown. If the information on her death record is correct, she was born in 1874. Youther was born in 1886, which indicates that she was twelve years old at the time of his birth.

According to the tax and deed records in the Bibb County, Georgia, probate court, she was married twice. The first marriage was with James Perryman, with whom she had two sons, Major Charles Perryman and James Perryman Jr. Lizzie and James Perryman purchased a home in Macon, in Bibb County, Georgia, where they lived until his death. Her second marriage was with John Smith.

At the time of Lizzie's death, she was a housewife. Her last-known address was 118 Rockhills Lane in Macon, Georgia. A funeral service was held at Hutchings Funeral Home, with burial at Lindwood Cemetery in Macon.

Children of Lizzie Smith and James Perryman are:

Youther Baldwin, born December 12, 1886, in Eatonton, in Putnam County, Georgia; died May 5, 1957, in Macon, Georgia. (He was James Perryman's stepchild.)

James Perryman, born 1895, date of death unknown.

Major Perryman, birth date unknown.

Generation No. 2

Youther Baldwin (Lizzie Baldwin Perryman Smith) was born December 12, 1886, in Eatonton, in Putnam County, Georgia, and died May 5, 1957, in Macon, Georgia. He married **Dora Ross**, daughter of Enoch Ross and Nancy Swift.

Notes for Youther Baldwin:

He lived at 1577 Woodliff Street in Pleasant Hill, one of the oldest communities in Macon. The community was organized in 1872 and covers about 430 acres—it is known for its honeysuckle and mimosa trees. Youther lived there in a Victorian-eclectic architecturally design house with his eighth wife, **Pinkie,** until his death at age seventy-one.

His burial site also is located in the Linwood Cemetery in Macon, Georgia. While doing my research, I read that Pinkie passed away on December 20, 1991, and is buried in Linwood Cemetery.

Notes for Dora Ross:

Dora was born to Enoch and Nancy Ross Swift; she was raised in and around Peach, Byron, and Houston counties. At the early age of 16, she became a mother. Later, she met and married Youther Baldwin. She was at the tender age of 36 years 8 months and 20 days, and the mother of five (with the youngest being 6 years of age), when she was beckoned by the angels to give up the fight.

On the afternoon of April 20, 1923, she could no longer hold on, and her life succumbed to bronchial asthma, which she had suffered with most of her life. Her burial site is located in the Swift Cemetery beside her mother's parents, Walton and Harriet Swift, in Byron, Georgia. (Georgia State Board Of Health, Bureau Of Vital Statistics, Certificate of Death file #11620.)

Children of Youther Baldwin and Dora Ross are:

Mary Lee Baldwin, born June 16, 1902, in Perry, Georgia; died March 6, 1985, in Jacksonville, Florida.

Luther Baldwin, born November 13, 1907, in Houston County, Georgia; died November 1, 1979, in Philadelphia, Pennsylvania.

Notes for Luther Baldwin:

Luke faithfully served on the trustee and deacon boards at the church where he was baptized, the Ebenezer Baptist Church in Macon. And he was an active member of the Prince Hall Masons (Central City Lodge No. 12, in Macon) for forty-one years. After relocating to Philadelphia, Pennsylvania, he became affiliated with the Liberty Baptist Church and also became very active with the 6100 Pine Street Civic Association (a neighborhood association).

At his homegoing service, his granddaughter Mary Ann Stewart paid a tribute to him that was evidence of her love. She read a poem she wrote in his honor simply called, "To Big Daddy." She related all the ways he had helped her, and she shared her love and devotion to him. Every word she spoke reflected the goodness of a man so loved by everyone whose life he touched. The entire church was brought to tears. Sandra Kleckley, his granddaughter-in-law, expressed her love in a beautiful rendition of the song "Beams of Heaven," and we felt his spirit there.

Cora Mae Baldwin, born December 22, 1909, in Perry, Georgia; died April 7, 1997, in

Macon, Georgia.

Walter Baldwin, born October 4, 1913, in Houston County, Georgia. He married Rebecca Brantley on August 5, 1934. No children were born to this union.

Walter Baldwin has one son, Curtis Baldwin.

Eugene Baldwin, born February 29, 1916, in Houston County, Georgia; died August 24,

1992, in Dublin, Georgia. He married Julia Mae Phelps on April 16, 1938, in Macon, Georgia.

No children were born to that union.

Notes for Eugene Baldwin:

Eugene Tablet Baldwin (Gene) was a member of New Hope Baptist Church in Macon, Georgia. He retired from Happ Brothers

Clothing Company, and he had also worked at WNEX Radio Station in Macon, Georgia. He was a member of the Good Samaritan Lodge and a World War II army veteran. Because of his deeds during service, he received two Bronze Stars and a good-conduct medal before receiving an honorable discharge. Gene was a patient at the Dublin VA hospital at the time of his death.

His wife preceded him in death. Family and friends joined at the House of God Church in Macon to bid him farewell. His burial site is located in the Bibb Mount Zion Baptist Church Cemetery in Macon, Georgia.

Generation No. 3

Mary Lee Baldwin (Youther Lizzie Baldwin Perryman Smith), born June 16, 1902, in Perry, Georgia; died March 6, 1985, in Jacksonville, Florida. She married Edgar Sims on April 20, 1942, in Macon, Georgia.

Notes for Mary Lee Baldwin:

Mary Lee was converted and baptized at an early age, becoming a member of the New Hope Baptist Church. John Smith and she united in Holy Matrimony. That marriage ended in divorce. Moving to

Macon, she found employment at Mckesson and Riley. She met and united in Holy Matrimony with Edgar Sims. No children were born to either union.

She joined the First Corinth Baptist Church and served faithfully as president of the Deaconess Board No. 1 for many years; president of District No. 1; president of the Senior Missionary Society; finance secretary of the Citywide Deaconess Union; and treasurer of the Sewing Circle.

At the time of her death, she was mother of the church, and she was financially and inspirationally rearing a grandniece, Barbara Denise Banks.

Burial site for Mary Lee Sims and Edgar Sims can be visited in the Mount Olive Cemetery in Jacksonville, Florida.

The epitaph given was "Servant of God, Well Done," by John Wesley, and her favorite poem, the Native American Ishi's "Poem for the Living."

Luther Baldwin (Youther, Lizzie Baldwin Perryman Smith) was born November 13, 1907, in Houston County, in Georgia, and died

November 1, 1979, in Philadelphia, Pennsylvania. He married **Mary**

Mims.

The funeral service was held on November 7, 1979, at Liberty

Baptist Church in Philadelphia, Pennsylvania. His burial site is

located in the White Chapel Cemetery in Pennsylvania.

Luther Baldwin and Mary Mims raised one boy and six girls:

Annie Baldwin.

Johnnie Mae Baldwin Lamar, born in Orlando, Florida; died April

1997, in King of

Prussia, Pennsylvania.

Lois Baldwin, born in Bibb County, Georgia; died September 7,

1951, in Bibb County.

Luther Baldwin Jr., born in Macon, Georgia.

Rosa Mae Baldwin, born May 5, 1921, in Macon, Georgia; died

April 1981, in Columbus, Ohio.

Ruth Baldwin, born February 25, 1928, in Macon, Georgia; died

January 1976, in

Philadelphia, Pennsylvania.

Carrie Mae Baldwin, born October 16, 1939, in Macon, Georgia; died February 25,

1988, in Philadelphia, Pennsylvania.

Cora Mae Baldwin (Youther, Lizzie Baldwin Perryman Smith) was born December 22, 1909, in Perry, Georgia, and died April 7, 1997, in Macon, Georgia. She married **Herry Banks** (son of **Cook Banks** and **Minnie Walker**) on February 28, 1928, in Macon, Georgia.

Her aunts and uncles were **Florence, Hattie, Mamie, Tommie, Enoch, Rosalee,** and **Florene**. Her grandparents were **Nancy Swift** (lived 1870–March 7, 1931) and **Enoch Ross** (lived 1853–December 28, 1932), and her great-grandparents were **Walter Swift** (born 1820–date of death unknown) and **Harriet Swift** (born 1840–date of death unknown). Cora Mae also had some cousins—**Amy, Bell,** and **Emma**.

Children of Cora Baldwin and Herry Banks are:

(See Banks family tree.)

Generation No. 4

Annie Baldwin (Luther, Youther, Lizzie Baldwin Perryman Smith). She married Henry Moten.

Children of Annie Baldwin and Henry Moton are:

John Irvin Mosley.

Bernard Moten.

Velton Moten.

Gary Moten.

Gregory Moten.

Carlton Moten.

Lannie Moten.

Johnnie Mae Baldwin (Luther, Youther, Lizzie Baldwin Perryman Smith) married **Milton Lamar** in 1941.

Child of Johnnie Baldwin and Milton Lamar is:

Mary Ann Lamar.

Lois Baldwin (Luther, Youther, Lizzie Baldwin Perryman Smith), born in Bibb County, Georgia; died September 7, 1951, in Bibb County. She married Ernest Holmes on August 1(year unknown).

Luther Baldwin Jr. (Luther, Youther, Lizzie Baldwin Perryman Smith) married **Alice Green**.

Children of Luther Baldwin and Alice Green are:

Pamela Marie Baldwin.

Luther Baldwin III.

Malcolm David Baldwin.

Rosa Mae Baldwin (Luther, Youther, Lizzie Baldwin Perryman Smith) married **Peter Clark**.

Child of Rosa Baldwin and Peter Clark is:

Mathis Kleckley Sr., born May 8, 1939; died 1998.

Ruth Baldwin (Luther, Youther, Lizzie Baldwin Perryman Smith) married **Samuel Adam Mays**, in Bibb County, Georgia.

Children of Ruth Baldwin and Samuel Mays are:

Chequeta Mays, born in Philadelphia, Pennsylvania.

Samuel Adam Mays Jr., born in Philadelphia, Pennsylvania.

Lois Mays, born in Philadelphia, Pennsylvania.

Carrie Mae Baldwin (Luther, Youther, Lizzie Baldwin Perryman Smith) married **Louis Willis**.

Notes for Carrie Mae Baldwin:

Carrie was a beautiful, devoted wife and mother. She was educated in Georgia's Bibb County school system and Fort Valley State College in Peach County. After completing her education, she moved to Philadelphia, Pennsylvania. Later, she was united in holy matrimony with Louis Willis; and from that union three children were born, one of them was a daughter who preceded her in death.

Her husband, two daughters—Deneen and Hope—family, and friends said goodbye to Carrie Mae on March 2, 1988, at Mount Carmel Baptist Church in Philadelphia. Her burial site is located in Northwood Cemetery in Pennsylvania.

Promises

"What God Hath Promised," by Annie J. Flint

The epitaph given was the one that begins, "Blessed sleep, Kindest minister to man …"

Children of Carrie Baldwin and Louis Willis are:

Carron Deneen Willis.

Hope Latanya Willis.

Harry Cook Banks *(See Banks family tree.)*

Joe Clarence Banks *(See Banks family tree.)*

Mary Frances Banks *(See Banks family tree.)*

Hubert Manuel Banks *(See Banks family tree.)*

Cora Mae Banks *(See Banks family tree.)*

Clara Lucille Banks *(See Banks family tree.)*

Generation No. 5

John Irvin Mosley (Annie Baldwin, Luther, Youther, Lizzie Baldwin Perryman Smith). He married **Mary Hammond**, who was born February 12, 1943, and died October 9, 1999.

Children of John Mosley and Mary are:

John Mosley.

Anthony Mosley.

Cristine Mosley.

Mark Mosley.

Mary Ann Lamar (Johnnie Mae Baldwin, Luther, Youther, Lizzie Baldwin Perryman Smith). She married **Robert Hayes**

Stewart, III February 10 (year unknown) in Philadelphia, Pennsylvania.

Children of Mary Lamar and Robert Stewart are:

Robert Stewart IV.

Kellee Lamar Stewart.

Mathis Kleckley Sr. (Rosa Mae Baldwin, Luther, Youther, Lizzie Baldwin Perryman Smith) was born May 8, 1939, and died 1998. He married **Sandra**. **Banks**

Notes for Mathis Kleckley Sr.:

Mathis's first marriage, to Katrina, ended in divorce. Two sons were born to this union.

Brad Kleckley.

Bryan Kleckley.

A few years after his divorce, he was united in holy matrimony with the beautiful and talented Sandra. He loved his wife so much, and she showered him with love and affection. This union bore no children.

Mathis realized he was gifted with a powerful voice and a love for God, and he began spreading the gospel in song. He was a very spiritual person, and he traveled near and far sharing his testimony of how good God is. He was a member of a gospel group when he was a young man living in Macon, Georgia. He later moved to Columbus, Ohio, and became a manager of the gospel group. Mathis had an unfortunate fall that caused his death.

Chequeta Mays (Ruth Baldwin, Luther, Youther, Lizzie Baldwin Perryman Smith) was born in Philadelphia, Pennsylvania. She married **James Simmons Jr.**

Children of Chequeta Mays and James Simmons are:

James Erasha Simmons.

Eron Simmons.

Temesha Jasmine Simmons.

Samuel Adam Mays Jr. (Ruth Baldwin, Luther, Youther, Lizzie Baldwin Perryman Smith) was born in Philadelphia, Pennsylvania. He married **Lynn Diane Brooks**.

Clara L. Chandler

Children of Samuel Mays and Lynn Brooks are:

Samuel Adams Mays III.

Curtis Mays.

Scott Mays.

Lois Mays (Ruth Baldwin, Luther, Youther, Lizzie Baldwin Perryman Smith) was born in Philadelphia, Pennsylvania. She married **Alonzo Sweeting**.

Children of Lois Mays and Alonzo Sweeting are:

ShaunTerrell Mays.

Lonnie Julius Sweeting.

Maurice Dante Sweeting.

Harry Cook Banks Jr. *(See Banks family tree.)*

Curtis Alan Banks *(See Banks family tree.)*

Christopher Darian Banks *(See Banks family tree.)*

Katherine Banks *(See Banks family tree.)*

Clarence J. Banks *(See Banks family tree.)*

Diane Harge *(See Banks family tree.)*

Rebecca Gayle Banks *(See Banks family tree.)*

166

Dorothy Jean Banks *(See Banks family tree.)*

Vivien Denise Banks *(See Banks family tree.)*

Marshell Stenson lll *(See Banks family tree.)*

Mary Adrienne Stenson *(See Banks family tree.)*

Roslin Banks *(See Banks family tree.)*

Hubert Manuel Banks, Jr. *(See Banks family tree.)*

Ken Banks *(See Banks family tree.)*

Sharon Bonita Banks *(See Banks family tree.)*

Barbara Denise Banks *(See Banks family tree.)*

Samuel Jerome Banks *(See Banks family tree.)*

Generation No. 6

Charrod Javon Banks *(See Banks family tree.)*

Demeterius Rashon Alston *(See Banks family tree.)*

Nikki TeCora Banks *(See Banks family tree.)*

Sarrina Raysha Banks *(See Banks family tree.)*

Other Relatives

I pray that this book will bring some closure to those who were not afforded the opportunity to meet with the grandest elders in whose

Clara L. Chandler

honor this book is written. Please be kind and remember that I stepped

out on this venture alone and with all good intentions. To God be the

glory.

With the passage of time also comes the passage of stories from

family history. In the time of early man, stories were told from

generation to generation, without the benefit of written record. Thus,

while much knowledge of ancestry was retained, much was indeed

lost. This book will furnish a brief—yet in-depth—history of my life

and family. It is for those too young to remember, for those who never

knew them, and to those not yet born.

Curtis Baldwin Jr., Nicole and baby Kiyah, Curtis Baldwin Sr. and Charles Davis

Josie Moran Family

Eunice, Charles Jr. & Lillie

Geneva Simmons

Lawanda, Robert, Cora & Louise

Mr. Sam Mays, daughter's & grandson

Hope, Kellee & Charles

Luther, Malcolm & Pamela

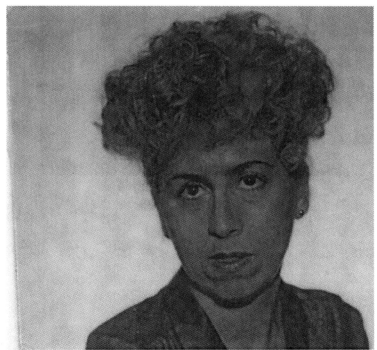

Giesla Bannister

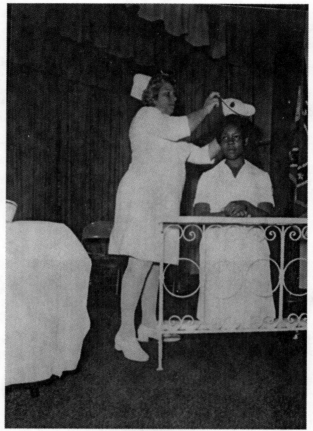

Janice Jolly being capped

Cora Mae Banks at age 85

Patricia Mosley

Luther Baldwin Jr.

Stenson Family

Kartika, Lauren & Joel

Scriven Family

Nikki TeCora & Anteiga

179

Harry & Emma Banks

Brandon, Lorraine & Harry Jr.

Curtis & Stacy Banks

Natasha, Wally, and Christopher

Althea, Clarence & Charrod Banks

Shawn Rice

Kenise and Krystyna Banks

Ken Banks

Hubert Banks Jr. & son Trevor

Roslin Banks

Hubert Banks Sr.

Cora Mae Ammons

Ammons Family

Willie & LaWanda Thomas on wedding day

Clara L. Chandler

Turonald & Elly Banks

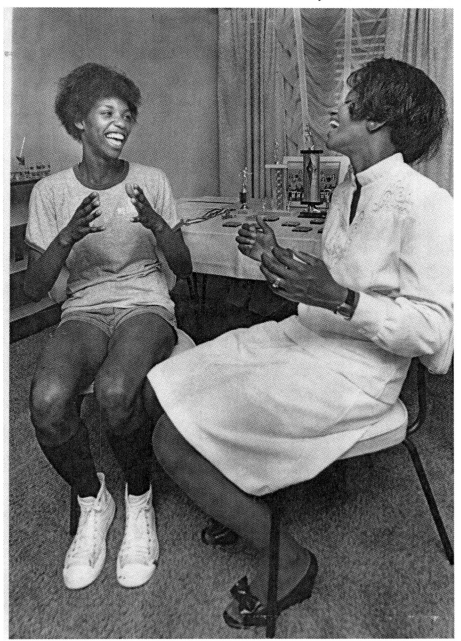

Cora Ammons & daughter Sharon Banks laughing in sign language

Barbara Denise Banks

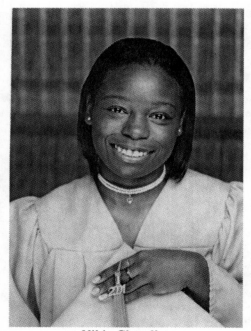

Nikia Chandler

Samuel & Claudette Banks

Barbara, Louis Sr., Sarrina & Elijah

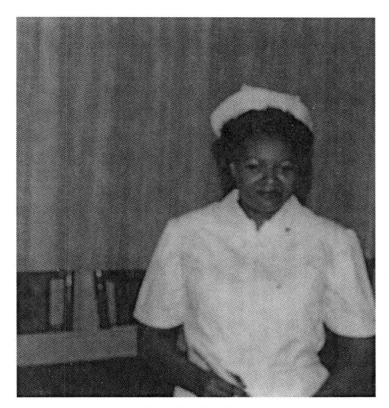

Clara L. Chandler

Samuel & Claudette Banks on wedding day

Omarri Saunders & Louis Banks, Jr.

William Marcus Banks

Clara L. Chandler

Hugh and Clara on a cruise

Sallie Jones Family

Malik Jones & Javron Banks

Sarrina, Ron & Louis Banks Sr.

Mattie Ross Felton

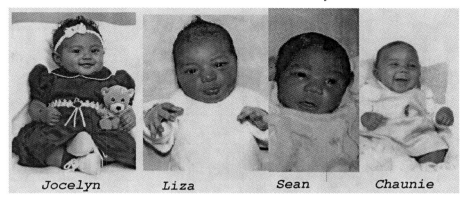

Jocelyn   Liza   Sean   Chaunie

Pamela, Alice & Sarah

About the Author:

Clara Lucille Banks Chandler has resided in the suburbs of Washington, D.C., for the past twenty-seven years. She lives there with her husband, Hugh D. Chandler, who retired after working in several departments of the federal government. She is the mother of two children, grandmother of four, a great-grandmother of four, and a stepmother of six.

Clara grew up through high school in Macon, Georgia. Clara left her hometown of Macon, Georgia, in 1963 and continued her education at Apex Business School in Brooklyn, New York, and at National Medical\Business School in Alexander, Virginia. Clara went on to work in the Washington Metropolitan area in a variety of roles in the medical field until she retired in February of 2002. For more than a decade she has faithfully attended the New Macedonia Baptist Church in Washington, D.C.

She hopes that by writing this book she will inspire the youth of today to learn of their historical cultures, appreciate the struggles of their forefathers, and continue to keep their legacy alive.

They Weathered the Storm is the first book written by Clara. Among her many friends and relatives who made this book possible, she would also like to thank her editor, Mrs. Netty Kahan. Thank you Netty—your patience and editing skills are exceptional.